D0374529

Redeeming
HALLOWEEN

FOCUS ON THE FAMILY®

Redeeming HALLOWEEN

Celebrating Without Selling Out

Kim Wier & Pam McCune

TYNDALE

Tyndale House Publishers, Wheaton, Illinois

REDEEMING HALLOWEEN
Copyright © 2004 by Kim Wier and Pam McCune.
All rights reserved. International copyright secured.

ISBN: 1-58997-155-8

A Focus on the Family book published by Tyndale House Publishers,
Wheaton, Illinois.

All Scripture quotations, unless otherwise indicated, are taken from the *Holy
Bible, New International Version®*. NIV®. Copyright © 1973, 1978, 1984 by
International Bible Society. Used by permission of Zondervan Publishing
House. All rights reserved.

Scripture quotations marked (NKJV) are taken from the *New King James
Version*. Copyright © 1982 by Thomas Nelson, Inc. Used by permission.
All rights reserved.

Scripture quotations marked (NASB) are taken from the *New American
Standard Bible®*. Copyright © 1960, 1962, 1963, 1968, 1971, 1972, 1973,
1975, 1977, 1995 by The Lockman Foundation. Used by permission.
(www.Lockman.org).

No part of this publication may be reproduced, stored in a retrieval system, or
transmitted in any form or by any means—electronic, mechanical, photocopy,
recording, or otherwise—without prior permission of the publisher.

Focus on the Family books are available at special quantity discounts when
purchased in bulk by corporations, organizations, churches, or groups. For
more information, contact: Focus on the Family, 8605 Explorer Drive,
Colorado Springs, CO 80920; or phone (800) 932-9123.

Library of Congress Cataloging-in-Publication Data

Wier, Kim.
  Redeeming Halloween : celebrating without selling out / Kim Wier and Pam
McCune.
      p. cm. — (Focus on the Family)
  ISBN 1-58997-155-8
  1. Halloween—Religious aspects—Christianity. I. McCune, Pam. II. Title.
III. Focus on the Family presents.
  GT4965.W48 2004
  394.2646—dc22   2004005652

Cover design: Amy Kiechlin
Cover copy: Joy Olson
Cover photo: Photodisc
Interiors: Angela Barnes

Printed in the United States of America
04 05 06 07 08/10 9 8 7 6 5 4 3 2 1

CONTENTS

IN MEMORY
Of "the leader who went before"
Dr. Bill Bright
who lived full of faith and died full of faith
praicing God to the last labored breath,
May I imitate your faith in life as well as death:
Running well and finishing well!
—Pam

To the most precious faith heroes I know:
my family
For my grandpa, Jay Owens, who has been savoring the face
of God for nearly 25 years, yet whose faith still inspires me.
For Grandma, Winifred Owens, whose faith
is ever fresh, even in the sunset of life.
And for all the Hembree family, past and present, who have
walked in unwavering faith in Christ and Christ alone.
What an incredible legacy!
—Kim

ACKNOWLEDGMENTS

How thankful we are to our heavenly Father for showing us so much about Himself through the process of this book. We hope that as you read, you find throughout the pages the fingerprints of God. It is because of His love and faithfulness through Jesus Christ that we desire to celebrate, communicate, and commemorate in this and every season.

What a privilege it is for us to partner with the amazing men and women at Focus on the Family who believe so strongly in the mission of helping families. Most especially thanks to those who had a vision for this project: Mark Maddox, Kathy Davis, Mick Silva, and Charles Hickmott. Charles, you have been a most appreciated friend, encourager, visionary, intermediary, and advocate. Thank you for sharing your many gifts with us and so many others.

SPECIAL THANKS FROM PAM

Jerry & Sue McCune Sr.—thank you for making this book possible by packing up and driving five hours to keep the kids on a moment's notice. You are Grandparents of the Year in my book.

Sandra Hancock & Diane Jones—what an impact you have made by modeling the spirit of giving on Halloween especially with dollars to my children, though it's your friendship that's priceless!

Justin & Heather Beadles—thank you for being a bright light on Halloween and such generous givers. Madison and Connor will never forget how "Pastor Justin gave us two handfuls of candy."

Natalie Lark & Angela Ebert—I truly appreciate your listening and praying me through my faithless moments. How did you always know the exact day when I needed your call? You both model listening to the Spirit of God intently and then acting on what you hear. When I grow up, I want to be like you!

The fifth- and sixth-grade girls at Grace Bible Church, Nacogdoches—I love your enthusiasm for giving. You are pretty good at sneaking around, too.

My precious family, Frank and Barbara Clarkson; David, Cam, Hayley, and Heather Sanders; Steve, Marilyn, Shaun, and Kyle Clarkson—life has always been easy to celebrate with you being part of it.

Madison & Connor McCune—I enjoy the season most of all because I spend it with you! Thank you for all your prayers and patience as I met deadlines.

Jerry McCune—You are the one. Without you this book would not be written, and my life would be lacking. I love you!

To the many faithful before me: Nana Cook, Georgia Blythe, Tim Pierce, Lori Paul, Lynn Kessler, Steve and Sarah Pogue, Sharon Diamond, Bev Morris, Nancy Cagle, and many more—thank you for living a life worth imitating. You have left your mark in my life.

SPECIAL THANKS FROM KIM

I look to the past and I am inspired. I look to the future and I dream. Yet it is the ones I look to in eternity who make my heart soar and put the wind beneath my wings.

My husband, Tony—Before every dream you say, "You can do it!" Through every disappointment you say, "Try again." In every circumstance you declare, "I love you." Thanks for being my dish washing, lawn mowing, shirt ironing, child loving, pile overlooking, wage earning, Sunday school teaching faith hero, here and now!

My man-boy Chase—My heart soars as I watch you test your own wings. You are my teen superhero with the power to change the world one decision at a time. Thanks for not just letting me in your world, but opening the door wide!

My joy-boy Bailey—Your tender heart and compassion are of heroic proportions and your passion for life is contagious. Thanks for modeling peacemaking, forgiveness, joy, and unconditional acceptance. Your heart for the underdog strengthens the weak and encourages the fainthearted. I am changed because of you.

My passionate princess Hannah—What an awesome and fearful thing to look into your eyes and see myself reflected. How proud I am that you already exceed me in every way because you continually make God the hero of your heart. I am challenged to be better so that you can follow me in confidence. Thank you for being my cheerleader.

You have each allowed me to write your stories, tell some of your secrets, and share your lives publicly that Christ would receive the glory. For Him you have literally made yourselves an open book. Thank you.

My heart also overflows to those who have put wind beneath the wings of Engaging Women Ministries, so that Christ would be known everywhere in every way.

Dr. Nick and Jade Schwedock and David Draper—your trust is a great gift.

My friends at KSWP/KAVX Radio—for all the ways you enable Engaging Women Radio, encourage and equip me, and are a faithful voice in the Piney Woods wilderness.

Our new friends at Family Life Ministries who have helped us share Christ in new ways.

Those in AWSA and CLASS who are heroes every day in

their own ministry circles but who take time to encourage, equip, and inspire others (like me) to press on toward the goal. Marita Littauer and Linda Evans Shepherd: Your leadership is bearing fruit. Thanks for rallying the estrogen troops.

To Grandma Linda who continually keeps Chase, Bailey, and Hannah from being orphaned when I'm away. A mother's job is never done. I will always need you.

To Grandpa John for cheering loudly enough for both of us when I couldn't be on the sidelines of every event. You are leaving a lasting legacy.

INTRODUCTION

We are so proud of you! You walked into a bookstore, and in front of God and everybody, you bought a book that has the word *Halloween* in the title! We won't ask if you hid it between the other really "spiritual" items you carried to the checkout counter. The point is you did it! (Either that or your mother-in-law sent you this book because she doesn't understand why you won't let her grandchildren go trick-or-treating.)

Like Pam and I, you may remember the days when the word *Halloween* didn't part a crowd like Moses parting the Red Sea. Back in the good ol' days, the only thing Halloween divided was a set of old bedsheets for the sake of a "primo" ghost costume.

The most original outfit I ever wore was in the fourth grade. I even entered a local grocery store's costume contest that year. On my very own, I created a pretty good replica of a grandfather clock cut out of a long cardboard box. Once inside, its realism was enhanced by the "tick tock" of my tap shoes as I paraded across the grocery store's makeshift stage. One of the most thrilling moments of my childhood was when the store manager called out my name (it was Kimmy back then) and handed me $25 and a second-place ribbon to the applause of the Piggly Wiggly shoppers. What could be more innocent than that?

Then came the year of rumors that some lunatic had put rat poison in trick-or-treat candy and razor blades inside apples. No longer was our greatest concern a trip to the dentist. Instead, we were considering having our candy x-rayed. From there, it was just a matter of time until Halloween fell out of grace with the

Christian community. Nowadays the talk isn't so much about tainted candy, but about satanic influences and celebrating evil. Parents who once looked to Halloween as good clean fun find themselves torn between what it was for them as a child and what they fear it has become.

Instead of a holiday, Halloween has become the albatross around our necks. As parents, we want to remain faithful to God's call and not violate our consciences, but we also want to avoid being fanatics who hide from reality. In searching for that balance, some of us attempt to focus on the innocent aspects while keeping a healthy distance from anything questionable. Others try to ignore the holiday, making Halloween the proverbial elephant in the middle of the room. A few Christian families may jump in with both feet and allow children to experience Halloween as our culture does. How many of us, though, are truly comfortable with our decision? And why do we still wrestle with our consciences every time October 31 rolls around?

There just doesn't seem to be a solution that satisfactorily answers the challenge. "To Halloween or not to Halloween?" That is the question. By now we realize the answer is not simple.

Pam and I know firsthand how stressful the whole issue can be. Both of our families have struggled to answer that question over the years, and in the process we have made mistakes, lost sleep, and gained a few gray hairs. Through our journey, though, God has revealed some truths about Halloween, our opportunity as His witnesses, and His greater plan of redemption.

We're excited to share what we've discovered on our emotional roller-coaster ride through Halloween. It's our hope that our experiences and this book will provide you with the facts, ideas, and inspiration that will help you make the best choices for your family. Together we will discover the redeeming origins of Halloween and answer that elusive question, "Can I really celebrate without selling out?"

TO HALLOWEEN OR NOT TO HALLOWEEN?

The Great Halloween Debate

Contrary to popular belief, the most prevalent emotion of the Halloween season is not fear. It's guilt—guilt, guilt, and more guilt. As parents, either we feel guilty because we're depriving our children of enjoying the holiday, or we feel guilty for not depriving them when our convictions tell us we should. It isn't always self imposed guilt either. There's no shortage of people ready to give an opinion or make a judgment about how we should deal with Halloween.

This is where fear becomes an issue—and not of black cats or goblins or creatures in the night. Rather, a fear of the creatures in the pews across from us. We're terrified of being judged for how we spend October 31. For those who feel participation in some aspects of the holiday is harmless, they must pass the gauntlet of well-meaning friends and family armed with tracts and literature warning of Halloween's dangers, from "God will smite you!" to "Satan will gain a foothold."

On the other hand, if we decide to stay out of the world's sugar-crazed revelry, we might be accused of being judgmental ourselves. If perchance we should escape either perspective, we only have to turn on a Christian radio station to get an opinion. That's where I first encountered the Great Halloween Debate.

The whole controversy became a reality for us when my son Chase was just two years old. During that season of life I was a talk-radio junkie. As a young mom, talk radio was my intellectual reprieve from *Barney* and *Thomas the Tank Engine*. During his afternoon nap, I folded the never-ending pile of laundry and solved all the world's problems by debating with the boom box. It was a somewhat one-sided conversation, but for that 60 minutes, I was able to "converse" with something that didn't spill, whine, or break anything.

That October, the topic of every program was Halloween. As hosts and guests debated the pros and cons (few pros and many cons), I grew increasingly concerned over what I was hearing: the occult, dark origins, and the dangers of participating in a celebration of evil. Some of the arguments were far-fetched, but many seemed legitimate. So I decided to do a little more investigating by diving headfirst into the hullabaloo.

I didn't have to look very far to find that many Christians agreed with the idea that Halloween ought to be avoided altogether. It just so happened that none of those experts were my friends. At the time, most of my friends were busy making costumes and stocking up on candy. The compromise for most of the families I knew was that along with the Snickers and Milky Ways, they would also give out a small cartoon tract about Jesus.

Even though that option sounded reasonable, as my husband, Tony, and I prayed about allowing little Chase out on the streets with only his Power Ranger gloves for protection, we didn't feel at peace with any decision. Instead, since he was still so young, we decided that rather than push aside our doubts we would simply not participate that year and revisit the issue again later.

By the next October, we had a new baby in the house, and Chase's friends were talking about trick-or-treating. The pressure was on, but again, we did nothing. Eventually we knew a decision would have to be made on the merits of what we felt was right before the Lord for our family. It finally came down to this: If there was any chance that what we were doing would dishonor God, we had to abstain. Since we just didn't know how God viewed the whole issue, Halloween was out for us.

Unfortunately, that didn't end the controversy. Every year as the holiday rolled around, at least one of my three children would ask again, "Mom, why don't we celebrate Halloween?"

As I'd scroll through the list of reasons, I tried to convince myself as much as them that ours was the right choice. Yet for practical reasons, we still needed something to do on the night when everyone else was having fun.

That decision was even harder than the first.

One year we stayed home and handed out candy and crossword puzzles about Jesus to a parade of superheroes and masked raiders. But that was just too much for our kids, longing to join in the fun. The next year we turned out all our lights and quietly watched a movie in the back room. We felt like fugitives in our own home. It just felt wrong to hide from the world. Finally the next year we decided we would have our own night out on Halloween as a family, but even that was a challenge. At every restaurant and every store, employees were dressed and ready to hand out candy and wish us "Happy Halloween." There was simply no getting away from the Halloween onslaught—the American holiday second only to Christmas in participation and revenue according to a press release by the National Retail Federation (October 1, 2002).

I happily admit that I was always glad when November 1 arrived because I didn't have to think about Halloween for another 364 days! I wouldn't have to decide if we should stay in or go out. I wouldn't have to console my confused and frustrated children. I wouldn't have to feel guilty and struggle to sort out

God's will in this gray area. I could go back to focusing on less complex problems—like world peace.

We are under no delusion that Christian families who do choose to celebrate Halloween have any easier time. Most of them just hope to make it through the night without running into anyone they know, especially their church friends. You can talk to a brother or sister in Christ about anything, but you will never hear them swapping costume ideas before the morning worship service. It's not sacrilege, but it might be close. Instead, committed Christians who "do Halloween" generally do it on the lam, feeling it's the less "spiritual" choice, even as they forge ahead in clown makeup or a movie-star mask. They're staying the course, but they're still making sure that course doesn't lead by the pastor's house.

Pam's family has experienced both sides over the years as well:

> Thank goodness I had no idea of the controversy as a child. Halloween was always a blast. It was like having a neighborhood progressive dessert. The more places you visited, the better position you were in when you laid out all your candy for the trading game. What memories! I can't remember when Halloween took on a new meaning, but years before we had children, my husband and I began to wrestle with the question, Is it evil or not? As staff with Campus Crusade for Christ, Jerry and I wondered how to lead in this area. We generally stayed away from the controversy itself and instead hosted outreach events such as "Happy October 31" parties. We felt good about making it an opportunity to reach out. Halloween was just one more tool for spreading the gospel. We still leaned toward the belief that the day had more evil potential than good, but I never shied away from a friendly debate on the subject.

Eventually, when we had children, all those theoretical arguments about what should be done became *real* questions. When our daughter, Madison, began to notice October 31, we had to begin practicing what we preached. If it was evil we couldn't join in just because we had kids, could we? So we turned out all the lights and hid. My very logical daughter, however, wanted a reasonable explanation for why we were hiding. We always try to use Scripture rather than a blanket "because I said so" rationale. In this case, however, we couldn't find any "hiding" verses.

So the next year, we turned on our lights and gave out the best candy with a spiritual comic book to all the ghouls and goblins. We even let our own kids dress up and hand out the candy, so long as they weren't actually participating in the "evilness" of the day. But Madison pressed the issue. "How come giving candy isn't evil, but *getting* candy is?" Jerry, caught off guard by her question, simply said we didn't want to actually participate in celebrating Satan's day.

Not long after we had visited my sister Cam's family, who does celebrate Halloween, I got a phone call from Cam. Apparently Madison had spent some time "educating" her cousins about the holiday. "Pam, Madison had a conversation with Heather about Halloween, and now my daughter is asking me why we celebrate Satan if we love God. Pam, do you really think my family is celebrating Satan because we trick-or-treat?"

What an eye-opener! I'm still apologizing for that one. The truth is, we were struggling. So once again, we reevaluated how we might balance our convictions with love. The search for an answer was on again. We'd gone to carnivals and not gone to carnivals. We'd trick-or-treated and not trick-or-treated. We'd dressed as Bible characters and as superheroes. No matter what we did, it didn't feel right. Still, we were committed to engaging our culture and being lights in the darkness, which meant taking some flak from our Christian friends. In the end, we felt we simply had declared an uneasy truce with Halloween and would rather not be put in the position of defending it. There was just too much ammunition on the side of avoiding the evil day. It was not a battle we wanted to fight.

Does any of that sound familiar? Does Halloween seem more a stumbling block than a holiday in your family? Our own families have never felt peace that we were making the most God-honoring, spiritually profitable choice. We were just coping in our own ways, making the best out of a regrettable situation, like a boy kissing his mother in front of friends. He doesn't want to, but since there is no escape, he just prays no one's watching.

How curious that those who share the mind of Christ can't share a compatible view of one day on the calendar. As Pam and I consoled each other over our predicaments, we also compared notes regarding the facts, as we knew them, about Halloween. To our surprise, what we found was that we both had separate versions of Halloween's origin. She had heard one thing; I had heard another. One source contradicted another. We couldn't discuss the facts because we didn't know whose "facts" were true.

In spite of the differences, we'd both come across general information that convinced us of Halloween's pagan origins. We both had literature warning that participating would compromise our faith. The "documented" facts, however, ranged widely—and wildly. It was apparent someone's research was wrong. That made us curious. What *was* the real truth? We weren't so sure we knew anymore.

Thus began our journey for the "rest of the story." Halloween had caused us both so much grief—and guilt—we were determined, once and for all, to get to the bottom of it. What we learned on our journey back was more surprising than we'd imagined. To our amazement, it did more than answer our questions about the holiday. The story we discovered strengthened our faith, humbled us before God, and revealed anew the glory of Jesus Christ. Far from divisive, what we discovered was a place where all Christians—of any denomination—can find agreement. For you see, the story of Halloween begins at the foot of the cross. We invite you now to hear the rest of the story.

HALLOWEEN'S TRUE STORY

Kim Introduces Halloween

I n the fifteenth year of the reign of Tiberius Caesar—when Pontius Pilate was governor of Judea . . ." (Luke 3:1).

So begins the biblical account of the public ministry of Jesus Christ from the book of Luke—and so is found the seed of Halloween.

In a time when the known world was ruled by Rome, an oppressive dominion of a one-world government, the Son of God came to change that world forever. An unknown man from Galilee began to teach about a new kingdom. To many, His seemed like words of anarchy. Few understood their real meaning, and many were anxious for a new king to come and replace the current, famously brutal regime. Patiently, Jesus continued to share the spiritual reality behind His words.

At the time, it seemed few were listening. Yet those who were paying attention heard words they would never forget, words that one day would echo loudly. Jesus said His followers would suffer for His sake, be abused by men, and even be killed for proclaiming the truth (Matthew 10:16-39). It would be by the faithfulness of the men and women who endured such persecution that God would spread the gospel and firmly plant the church of Jesus Christ for all time. Christ had foretold it, and for the first three hundred years after His ascension into heaven, that suffering would be unparalleled.

Persecution came first from the Jews, then from the Gentiles under the direction of the Roman government. Defenseless Christians became the target of the state's cruelest and most persistent campaign of extermination. The culture served many gods, especially the god of self-indulgence, and Christianity was an affront to the deities of Rome. Christians were heretics, the easy target of blame whenever a situation arose. If it was drought, the Christians had offended the rain god. If fire, or earthquake, or flood, the gods were angry at the Christians' unwillingness to sacrifice to them. Even military misfortunes were these stubborn people's doing.

Beginning with Nero, wave after wave of persecution swept over the budding church. Eventually no excuse was needed. Christians subverted the state religion—paganism—and became a thorn in Rome's side. The empire's answer was torture. For three hundred years, heathenism battled Christianity and compromise was impossible. Such opposing worldviews could not declare truce.

Ignatius, leader of the church in Antioch in A.D. 107, was a pupil of the apostle John. When Ignatius refused to renounce Christ, he was condemned to the lions. He was bound and taken to the capital where in Rome, Christians greeted and encouraged him, but they could not delay his divine appointment. On December 20, 107, still refusing to deny his Lord, Ignatius was thrown into the amphitheater and torn apart by wild animals as the crowd cheered.

Though events like this were common, they did not have the effect Rome desired. Pagans who witnessed the courage and conviction of Ignatius and others like him were drawn to the faith. Miraculous stories of converts were recorded as a result of such steadfast faith. Miraculous too are the stories of God's grace to those who endured.

Another friend and student of the apostle John for some 20 years, Polycarp, endured an excruciating death with praise on his lips. Commanded to deny Christ, he responded, "Eighty-six years I have served the Lord Jesus Christ, and He never once wronged me. How can I blaspheme my King who has saved me?" Polycarp was sentenced to be burned at the stake. Amid the flames, eyewitnesses recorded his praise to God, that he could "be counted among His martyrs, to drink the cup of Christ's suffering, unto the eternal resurrection of the soul and the body in the incorruption of the Holy Spirit." Witnesses said the flames seemed not to touch him, but only to refine him, and an executioner was required to kill him with a sword, as the fire would not. Those present reported that as the fire burned, a sweet aroma filled the stadium. The account served to strengthen the faith of believers.

A young mother, Perpetua, refused to deny the name of Jesus. Ignoring the pleas of her unbelieving father and frantic appeals to think of her young baby, she chose death and the promise of eternal life.

A group of 40 Roman soldiers stood together in their refusal to offer sacrifices to the Roman gods. Though they would lose their military status, they would not deny Christ. The furious Roman governor condemned them to be stripped and placed in the center of a frozen lake, surrounded by soldiers and tubs of hot water. Taunted to deny Christ and be permitted to climb into the warm tubs, only one of the 40 weakened. When a guard saw that man's denial, he grieved and he himself was converted on the spot. "I am a Christian!" he shouted, stripping off his uniform and taking the man's place to die with his new brothers on the frozen lake.

Many hearts came to faith, not in spite of these stories, but because of them.

Still, the lengths to which the government would go to force

Christians to deny their Savior seemed endless. The methods of torture have been unparalleled in human history. Strangled, beheaded, gouged, beaten, racked, boiled in oil, melted on hot iron plates, burned at the stake, fed to lions and bears, and crucified, men, women, and children went to their deaths praising God. Outsiders, amazed at the grace and often the joy with which Christians faced and endured death, discovered for themselves the salvation of Christ. In the face of unspeakable evil, the church grew. Even when Christians had no civil rights, their churches and Scriptures burned, and property confiscated, the church persevered, continuing to bear witness to the truth of Christ.

At last, a final attempt to wipe out this "unofficial sect" was made. Obvious that Christians would never be dissuaded, by A.D. 311 the supremacy of Christianity was clear. That year, an edict of toleration was issued, calling not only for an end to persecution, but also for the protection of Christians to meet together in worship. Its security was truly sealed, however, with the public conversion of Rome's emperor, Constantine, in the year A.D. 313. Within a short time, Constantine would declare Christianity the official religion of the Roman Empire, and thus the known world. God had indeed had a plan.

How is it that Christianity survived those three hundred years of horror? Philip Schaff, the nineteenth-century church historian, wrote, "To these protracted and cruel persecutions the church opposed no revolutionary violence, no carnal resistance, but the moral heroism of suffering and dying for the truth. But this very heroism was the fairest ornament and staunchest weapon. In this very heroism, she proved herself worthy of her divine Founder, who submitted to the death of the cross for the salvation of the world, and even prayed that His murderers might be forgiven." As Tertullian, a second-century martyr, rightly proclaimed to the Roman officials who sentenced him to death, "Rack, torture, grind us to powder. Our numbers increase in proportion as you mow us down. The blood of martyrs is the harvest seed [of the church]."

We are all part of that universal church—no matter the denominational label. As those who believe in salvation through Christ alone, we owe a debt of honor to the faithfulness of those who stood firm in the face of death and established the church.

As the church stepped into a new position of worldly honor, these martyrs were officially recognized. Special days were set aside to remember the individuals who had suffered and died for the love of their Savior. The list, though, was too long. There were not enough days on the calendar. Eventually one day was set aside for remembrance. In A.D. 610, the church dedicated May 13 as All Saints' Day. The "holy day" was added to other Christian festivals already being celebrated, namely Christmas, Easter, and Pentecost. Also known as All Hallows, May 13 was the day the festival was celebrated for over one hundred years.

Then in A.D. 741, All Hallows, or All Saints' Day, found a new home on the calendar. At that time there were concerns about the growing popularity of a pagan festival held on November 1, known as Samhain (pronounced "sow-en"). Dating back to the Celts and Druids, this pagan festival was beginning to have an influence even within the Christian community. To counteract this, the church turned to a previously successful strategy of claiming the date as their own. As in the case of Christmas, the celebration of Jesus' birth was assigned December 25 because that was the date pagans were celebrating the winter solstice.

This time, Samhain, the pagan festival of death, was replaced with All Saints' Day. Borrowing from the Jewish tradition of preparing for significant festivals, the Christian church reserved the day before the religious festival as a sacred time. October 31 was then set aside as an evening of preparation called "All Hallow 'een," or "the eve of the holy ones." Together, they created a meaningful time for the church to remember the early martyrs.

What happened to this church festival from that time until the present is where most of the debate rages. There is no denying that it did not endure as a significant religious holiday in the same way Christmas did, but neither has it faded into complete obscurity. Many other church-honored dates have faded away, yet Halloween and All Saints' Day have been preserved. Unfortunately, most don't realize the original intent of our church fathers. Though their reason for establishing the holiday is undeniable, over the years many cultures have influenced our current Halloween.

Remembering Hebrews 13:7, the church fathers believed in the value of honoring faithful men and women: "Remember your leaders, who spoke the word of God to you. Consider the outcome of their way of life and imitate their faith." There was, and still is, much to imitate in the lives of not only those who died a martyr's death, but also those who lived out lives full of faith. The Bible is replete with such stories.

One of the greatest examples of a martyr who brought honor to God comes from Acts 7 and the story of Stephen, the first believer recorded who died for his belief in Jesus Christ. The record shows Stephen's stand for Christ, his appeal for his accusers to believe, and his steadfastness as stones were hurled at his body. Yet even as the mob seized him, "Stephen, full of the Holy Spirit, looked up to heaven and saw the glory of God, and Jesus standing at the right hand of God. 'Look,' he said, 'I see heaven open and the Son of Man standing at the right hand of God'" (Acts 7:55-56). As the stones continued to fall, Stephen's last words, "Lord, do not hold this sin against them" (Acts 7:60), echo Christ's on the cross.

Why did God want this recorded for all time—the death of a mere man whose blood cannot save, who was neither sinless nor able to conquer sin? For the same reason He inspired accounts of not only Stephen's fellow martyrs, James (Acts 12:2),

Abel (Luke 11:51), John the Baptist (Mark 6:27), and Zechariah (2 Chronicles 24:21), but also those who lived by faith, including Enoch, Noah, Abraham, Isaac, Jacob, Moses, Joseph, and Rahab (see Hebrews 11).

"These were all commended for their faith" (Hebrews 11:39), their stories preserved so that we might "consider the outcome of their way of life and imitate their faith" (Hebrews 13:7).

Praise God such faith does not end with that list! The following three hundred years continued to see men, women, and children inducted into that same hall of faith. Nor did the list end with the legitimizing of Christianity. In every generation, followers of Jesus Christ have had their faith put to the test, without relenting, without recanting, and without compromising, even in the face of death.

That is what the night of Halloween was established to contemplate and celebrate.

No one can deny such a cause is worthy of Christian participation. Yet the argument remains that the season has become so distorted, it has gone beyond redemption. Believe it or not, at one time the same argument was made about Christmas. In the seventeenth century, many Protestants decided that true believers should not recognize Christmas because of its ties to pagan roots, and because it was seen as an exclusively Catholic holiday. In 1620, the Pilgrims began unloading the Mayflower on Christmas Day as a statement that they would not participate in such an evil holiday. Even today, there are some who reject Easter, what many consider the Christian church's most holy holiday, because of its supposed early pagan ties. To both groups, these holidays seem unredeemable.

Unless the primary work of God in the world is understood, we will continue to struggle with the same dilemma. It is clear from the Word of God that redemption is God's primary work. Since the fall of man in the Garden of Eden, every act of

God the Father, the Son, and the Holy Spirit has centered on the task of redeeming something lost. It is because of that work that empty relationships are restored, empty work is made eternal, and empty ritual becomes an act of spiritual worship. "For you know that it was not with perishable things such as silver or gold that you were redeemed from *the empty way of life handed down to you from your forefathers,* but with the precious blood of Christ" (1 Peter 1:18-19, emphasis added).

Just because a worthless legacy was passed down from those who went before does not mean it is irredeemable. The blood of Christ has the power to redeem all worthless things, whether that's Halloween or another "empty way of life handed down from our forefathers." Many of us can look at the redeemed places in our own lives and make that argument from firsthand experience.

If Halloween is just one more empty way of life in your family, we challenge you to consider the power of the blood of Christ, which brings worth out of something worthless. Even if it seems an insignificant place to take an eternal stand, remember: "God chose the foolish things of the world to shame the wise; God chose the weak things of the world to shame the strong. He chose the lowly things of this world and the despised things— and the things that are not—to nullify the things that are, so that no one may boast before him" (1 Corinthians 1:27-29).

You may think it is foolish, even impossible, but that is all the better, for when He accomplishes it, you will only be able to "boast in the Lord" (1 Corinthians 1:31). We have discovered that in the case of Halloween, the truth really can set you free: free from guilt, free from fear, and free to celebrate the power and goodness of God.

This book is not a plan for Halloween alternatives. We don't suggest you simply remake the world's version of Halloween. We hope to inspire you to take back the celebration that rightly belongs to the people of God and restore the purpose for which it was established.

It is actually quite simple, and as we have discovered, it is also fun and spiritually rewarding. By focusing on a truth worth *celebrating*, a message worth *communicating*, and people worth *commemorating*, Halloween can become more than a holiday. It will be a holy day.

You don't have to do every activity listed here. Some will work for your family, others will not, and there simply won't be enough time to do it all this year. So choose your favorite ideas and save the rest for next year. Who knows? Soon, you might actually begin *looking forward* to Halloween.

Best of all, once you discover the truth, you won't have to whisper the word *Halloween* anymore. You really can celebrate without selling out. Halloween, after all, is a holy word—for those willing to let Jesus redeem it.

Significant source of historical information taken from Philip Schaff, *History of the Christian Church* (Oak Harbor, Wash.: Logos Research Systems, Inc., 1997).

Celebrating
the Season

Put [your] hope in God,
who richly provides us with everything for our enjoyment.
—1 TIMOTHY 6:17

TRICK OR TREAT

Kim's and Pam's "Training Wheels"

Both the McCune and the Wier households love animals. Between us, we have had chickens, tarantulas, turtles, ferrets, birds, hamsters, gerbils, guinea pigs, rabbits, hermit crabs, fish, snakes, sundry insects, and of course, cats and dogs. Currently, 15 animals depend on us for their daily bread, kibble, seed, or frozen mice snacks. Admittedly it is considerable trouble to keep litter boxes cleaned, bowls filled, and furniture de-haired, but we think it's worth it.

Not only do our children get enjoyment from the variety of their pets, but they also learn a lot. For instance, if they forget to clean out the cage long enough, Mom will eventually get sick of the smell and do it for them while they're at school. They have discovered that a dog can go approximately three days without food before he drags the trash all over the yard looking for scraps. We all learned that if the snake gets loose in the house, it's better not to tell Dad about it until after it's recaptured!

What none of us have been very successful at is training our animals. No amount of effort has taught the dogs to fetch. No amount of discipline has stopped them from digging up the yard. The ferret will burrow into the clean laundry the first chance he gets, and the cat is continually compelled to sharpen her claws on the couch. The bird will not talk. The dogs will not stop chasing the cats, and the cats will not stop chasing the gerbils. Despite our best efforts, our wild kingdom operates more on its God-given instinct than on any of our methods.

Wouldn't it be wonderful if God had created our children with innate instincts about how to operate successfully in our families? They would know how to tie their shoes, make their beds, unload the dishwasher, and get along with their brothers and sisters automatically. They wouldn't need training to learn to share, ask forgiveness, or obey. Never again would we find them outside in a thunderstorm or barefoot in the snow. They would understand that you shouldn't catch a bee with your bare hands and that putting a penny in a light socket is not good. Best of all, teenagers would innately understand that parents are smarter than they look.

Reality is another story, however. God created mankind with the ability to learn and make choices rather than operate without free will. What that means for parents is that we need to provide lots of training while our children are young so that they will be prepared to operate successfully later in life. This is something most of us do all the time, often without even realizing it.

For example, most of us don't think about it, but before they are even six months old, we are training our kids how to drive, especially if they are boys. In the Wier household, we put Baby Chase in front of the toy steering wheel with the clown nose horn and let him go. As a toddler, he sat on Daddy's lap and gripped the wheel of the riding lawnmower, the engine rumbling beneath them. By seven he was playing motocross video games; by 10 he was driving a go-cart through the neighborhood. All along the way he was learning to "talk cars" with his dad.

Now that he's a teenager, all that training is paying off. As he gets behind the wheel to drive for real, it's amazing how prepared he is. As parents, we are clinging to the promise of Proverbs

22:6, "Train a child in the way he should go, and when he is old he will not turn from it." The way we trained him to go was within the speed limit, on the right side of the road, wearing his seatbelt, and with both hands on the steering wheel, not the radio. None of that comes by instinct (and certainly not from watching me drive!). Still, we trust that he will go the right way because all along his dad has been preparing him to make the right decisions.

Little girls are trained in much the same way. In the McCune family, "mommy training" happened quite by accident. My daughter simply followed my example. When my son, Connor, was born, I was overwhelmed with all of my added responsibilities, but they couldn't compare to the ones my daughter, Madison, mimicked at age three. While I took care of the new baby, she took care of Shea, Brooke, Layne, Beth, and Kendall—her baby dolls. When I needed to feed Connor, she retrieved all of her dolls and began feeding them as well. When I changed Connor's diapers, suddenly her girls needed changing also. At bath time they all squeezed into the sink together.

Most enlightening, however, was watching her methods of discipline for her babies.

"Now, you shouldn't hit each other. You will go to time out and get a spanking because I love you," she would scold.

I can't wait to see how she will someday use her experience of raising quintuplets.

In all of these areas, some specific "training wheels" are helping to steer our children straight. Spiritually, there are many things we are training our children as well. We want them to be committed to God's church so we take them to Sunday school every week. We want them to live godly lives as adults so we help them memorize God's Word. We want them to understand that all they possess belongs to God so even when they are children, we teach them to tithe from their allowance. It is also important to us that they grow up with a heart for reaching the lost with the gospel.. That attitude won't come naturally either. It, too, is an area that will require training.

Halloween can actually be a part of that process through the fun of trick-or-treating.

There are a variety of stories about the roots of trick-or-treating. The most authoritative describe a tradition called "mumming" where masqueraders went door-to-door for treats and performed simple plays in return for food or drinks. One story holds that the tricking element began in Ireland, on what became known as "mischief night." People would wander the town dressed in costumes, tipping over outhouses, unhinging fence gates, and engaging in other pranks. While none of these practices actually had religious influences, over time they may have been incorporated into Halloween.

When a large population of Irish immigrants came to America in the mid-1800s, they brought the tradition of mischief night with them. But by the turn of the century, it had become more than just a harmless night of pranks. By the 1920s, it had escalated into real destruction of homes and businesses. Neighborhood committees and even clubs such as the Boy Scouts began offering alternative ideas for the evening. To bring back the original fun of masqueraders going door-to-door, parents encouraged "good" children to dress up and visit shops and homes to receive treats. At each stop they gave the greeting "Trick or treat!" and a uniquely American event was born, with the result being that troublemakers were kept away. By the 1930s, the event had been dubbed "beggar's night," and it was being practiced all over the nation.

Who knows if those first city planners ever looked to God's Word for wisdom when dealing with "mischief night"? If they had, they would have found the very principle they were attempting to employ: "Everyone who does evil hates the light, and will not come into the light for fear that his deeds will be exposed" (John 3:20).

Bottom line, there is *nothing* inherently evil about trick-or-treating. Certainly every child likes to play dress up. Yet more than simply harmless fun, it can be a light to others in several ways. Simply by changing the focus when your children pick out costumes, you can change their focus to the needs of the spiritually lost.

Instead of allowing them to dress like superheroes or restricting them only to Bible heroes, we let our children dress like any character they want, as long as it represents a group they want to tell about Jesus. That doesn't necessarily limit the costume choices to people of other cultures and nationalities, though that's a great place to start brainstorming. But fair warning: children can get very creative—and you should encourage them in this as much as possible. To them, dressing like Elvis represents music stars who need Jesus. A football player (Connor's first choice) represents those living without Jesus in the sports culture. Last year, Bailey and Hannah were Ninjas and prayed for the lost in Asia. Madison was a 1920s flapper, and she prayed for the lost who hide in the darkness of dance clubs. The idea is to support their costume choice by getting them to think about people not like themselves, who need the gospel and who need someone to bring it to them.

Training our kids in the knowledge that they can reach others with the gospel is no small thing. How rewarding it will be years from now to discover that God fulfilled His promise that our children would not depart from reaching out to the lost through the "spiritual training wheels" we used on Halloween.

TIPS FOR TRICK-OR-TREATING WITH PURPOSE
🍁 Start early planning for the trick-or-treat experience so that your children will gain the greatest benefit from the evening.

❧ Brainstorm as a family the places and people where the gospel has been rejected. Be sure to allow the kids to offer as many ideas as they can. This time is important because even if they already have an idea how they would like to dress, it opens their thoughts to the need around the world.

❧ Let them share their ideas for costumes. If they have several, make a list and spend some time talking about how a costume could look.

❧ Keep an open mind! Even dressing as a sea creature could represent sailors or fishermen. They will enjoy the entire experience more if you allow them freedom to be creative. Remember, having fun is a legitimate goal and an important part of celebrating.

❧ Once they have chosen a costume idea, talk more specifically about the people being represented.

❧ Do some research together about the people your children's costumes represent. If they are from another country or culture, locate it on a map. Find out about customs, religious practices, and any other things that are distinctive to the group. Remind them that to reach someone, it is necessary to understand them.

❧ Talk about how people who have not accepted Jesus have been "tricked" into believing they don't need Him, but that God wants them to receive the greatest "treat," salvation through Jesus and eternal life in heaven.

❧ Make a list of some specific ways that your children can pray for that group of people to be prepared to hear the gospel. Include asking God to send workers into that mission field.

❧ Each night for a week before or after Halloween, pray with your children for their chosen country, people group, or culture.

❧ Look together at Jesus' commission given to us in Matthew 28:19: "Therefore go and make disciples of all nations, baptizing them in the name of the Father and of the Son and of the Holy Spirit." Take some time to talk about how each of us can obey that command right now and in the future.

❧ On Halloween night, as you prepare to send your children out to trick-or-treat, be sure to go over safety rules and accompany them from house to house.

❧ Remind them to say thank you at each place you visit. Have a great time enjoying a fun experience with your children that will result in spiritual training as well.

❧ After you arrive home and admire the abundance of candy, finish the night with a Scripture verse that promises sweet rewards for those who do God's work on earth. "It will be good for that servant whom the master finds doing [good things] when he returns" (Luke 12:43). And, "How beautiful are the feet of those who bring good news!" (Romans 10:15).

❧ Help your children see that while trick-or-treating can be a fun time one night a year, following God and sharing the good news of Jesus is an adventure that lasts a whole lifetime.

❧ Finish your trick-or-treat night with prayer as you tuck them into bed. Thank God that someone told you about Jesus, and ask Him to use your family to do the same for others.

LETTING IN THE LIGHT

Pam's Walk on the Wild Side

H igh adventure and travel—that was the life for me. Half of our belongings were stuffed into the car along with our three-year-old and 10-month-old kids as we left Texas behind, singing out, "California, here we come!" Why? To be a light to the world, of course. More specifically, we were going to be a light to the world of Santa Cruz, California.

Working with college students for the summer, training them to share their faith, and teaching them God's Word have always been our favorite responsibilities as staff members of Campus Crusade. Our summer project assignments have taken us to Panama City, Florida; Branson, Missouri; Yellowstone National Park; the Soviet Union; and even the Middle East. None of those travels, though, created the kind of anxiety brought on by Santa Cruz, California. Even though I began our journey saying, *Use me any way You want, Lord. I am ready*, I was soon on my face before Him, pleading, "I can't do this!"

As we were briefed about our new urban location, muffled alarms started going off in my mind, but despite the inner-city dangers that awaited us, I resolved to press ahead. When we were cautioned not to wear red in the neighborhood where we would be living because it was a gang color, I said I didn't look good in red anyway. I even managed to keep my nerve when we were told that it wasn't safe to go anywhere in the neighborhood alone. "The more the merrier" has always been my philosophy, so I was still okay. It wasn't until I actually got my first look at our new home for the summer that I began to have second thoughts.

Nothing could have prepared me for my first look at the Peter Pan Motel. Though it was to be turned over to our steadier-paying staff and students, our ministry headquarters for the next 12 weeks of summer was ordinarily a dwelling of drug dealers and "ladies of the night."

Arriving a week before the students to get the project ready, our first assignment was to transform that den of iniquity into accommodations that would not alarm our students. Instantly I knew I was in over my head. The rooms were covered in filth. Hypodermic needles were everywhere. Most of the items left behind were indescribable. I cleaned wearing three pairs of vinyl gloves, while also hovering protectively over my babies. Between the cleaning and guarding my children, I was completely over-whelmed. Over and over I prayed, *Lord, what am I doing in this evil place?*

On day four, when my 10-month-old baby's tongue broke out with white spots after playing in the dirt, I hit my breaking point. *Lord, this can't be what You have for my kids and me! We need to go home!*

Had it not been for what happened next, I might have done just that. In the midst of scrubbing, painting, planting, and haul-ing away loads of unspeakable trash, a miracle began to emerge. Out went the darkness, and in flooded the light. Hope and elbow grease had transformed the Peter Pan Motel into a mission. The day the students finally arrived was the brightest of all. With 80 college kids shining brightly for Jesus, the Peter Pan soon became the coolest place in town. Everyone wanted to hang out with us: youth from local churches, Campus Crusade student coworkers, and sometimes even strangers in the night looking for Trixi who "used to live here." We became a light in a dark place. It was truly a God thing.

For many Christians, Halloween may seem like the Peter Pan Motel: a hopeless pit of darkness from which they are ready to run—but it, too, has potential. While others are putting out skeletons, hanging cobwebs, and blasting spooky music, we can be a beacon of light in our neighborhoods. In keeping with our celebration of lives that shone into a dark world, we can send a message with what we choose to display.

"But you are a chosen people, a royal priesthood, a holy nation, a people belonging to God, that you may declare the praises of him who called you out of darkness into his wonderful light" (1 Peter 2:9).

Decorating is an important part of any seasonal celebration. It sets the mood, symbolically communicates a message, and adds some plain old fun. Like nativities at Christmastime, we can use lights at Halloween to testify to a needy world. We've listed several ideas to help you light up your neighborhood, so go for it! But be aware: Decorating is "coming out of the closet" as far as October 31 is concerned. You may just get the opportunity to explain why you chose to celebrate a holy Halloween.

Tips for Decorating with Light
Ways to Light Your Home

🍁 A great way to make an impact with light on Halloween is to string white Christmas lights on your house during October. Your home will stand in stark contrast to the dimness of others around you. (And after Halloween you will be ahead on your Christmas decorating!)

🍁 Make luminarias to line your walkway or drive. This is a simple and inexpensive way to light up your entryway.

- Buy brown or white paper lunch bags.
- Fill the bottom of each bag with two inches of sand.
- Place a small candle in the sand and light it at night.
- You can also use a hole punch or scissors to make crosses or other designs in the paper bag so that the light will illuminate the design. You could even write a letter on each bag to spell messages of hope.

🍁 Another way to light your home is to place lights in all of the windows that face the front. These can be electric candles or even real candles if they can be placed safely.

🍁 Rope lights are a great way to create a symbol on a rooftop. With just a couple of boxes of lights, you can create a cross that is the standout feature of your entire neighborhood. It will not go unnoticed on Halloween night.

Ways to Make Your Home a "Light"

🍁 Banners are another way to bring light to your neighborhood. Just as many churches create banners for special services, your family can work together to create a banner to display during Halloween. Even if you don't sew, you can still create a masterpiece. Here's how:

- Choose a phrase from Scripture that gives the message you want to communicate. Some examples are: "Jesus, the Light of the World"; "Jesus, the Bright and Morning Star"; "Perfect Love Casts Out Fear"; "Fear Not, I Am with You"; "Christ, the Rising Son"; "Father of Lights."
- Visit a fabric store and choose a sturdy cloth as the base of your banner. Be sure that you plan your measurements ahead of time so that you purchase the correct amount of cloth. For an outside display, on the front of your house for instance, we recommend a

banner that is about four feet by five feet. If cost is an issue, you can also use an old sheet.

- An inexpensive way to make the letters for the banner's message is to purchase felt by the yard. You can also use tempera paints if you have a steady hand.
- To make the banner special, buy a bag of remnant ribbon and notions and be creative in your decorating!
- Assembling the banner will require either a sewing machine, glue gun, or no-sew bonding sheets.
- Purchase a dowel rod from the hardware store in a size that will run the width of your finished banner.
- Begin by sewing or gluing a rod "pocket" at the top of your banner cloth through which your dowel rod can slide to hang the banner.
- If you don't want to sew the edges of the banner, cut them with pinking shears to give them a finished look.
- Use a tracing pencil to draw out the shape of your letters in the felt. Cut them out and attach them to your banner in one of the above-listed three ways.
- Embellish the banner with remnant pieces, glitter, or other decorations.
- Insert the dowel into the rod pocket of the banner.
- Attach a long piece of string to both ends of the rod (the rod should extend past the end of the pocket).
- Place a nail or hook securely where you want to hang your banner.
- Hang the banner by the string.

❧ Make a wreath for your front door that uses wheat and other harvest items. Display on the wreath the following verse: "Christ has indeed been raised from the dead, the firstfruits of those who have fallen asleep" (1 Corinthians 15:20).

❧ Since the harvest theme is so closely associated with the true message of Halloween, you may want to decorate with items such as hay bales, scarecrows, or pumpkins. We recommend that if you go this way you distinguish your decorations from those using harvest items as an alternative to Halloween by also displaying "harvest" verses with your decorations such as John 4:35, Matthew 9:37, or Luke 10:2.

PUMPKINS, LEGENDS, & LANTERNS

Kim's Veggie Woes

Vegetables are not evil."

No matter how many times my mom tried to convince me they were good, I just didn't believe it. As a kid, I was a picky eater, consuming a lot of grilled-cheese sandwiches. I didn't eat vegetables. Cooked carrots were slimy. Peas were pasty. Broccoli was bushy, and don't even get me started on beans. Corn was the only vegetable I would halfheartedly eat. After all, anything that produced popcorn couldn't be all bad. As for salads, a bowl of plain lettuce smothered in my mother's homemade Thousand Island dressing was as much as I could stand. Every meal I heard the tireless plea, "Just try one bite."

More times than she would care to recall, my mom worked to disguise the offensive veggies to slip them under my radar. She had to be pretty shrewd. Like any expert picky eater, my fork thoroughly dissected each bite.

These days, the veggie battle continues, but now I'm the one covertly trying to slip things past my children. No matter how I disguise them, they can detect a mushroom in any recipe. They have instincts to know if onions are lurking just under the surface of a sauce or if I have tried to slip peas into their beef stew. The only vegetables they consider truly edible are the ones smothered in butter or cheese, or that are commonly French fried.

Who can really blame them? After all, their first experiences with vegetables came in baby jars, mashed beyond recognition, devoid of seasoning. Is it any wonder they tried to spit out what appeared to have already been eaten once? Imagine the grueling ritual from their point of view: Day after day, they are restrained in a high chair while a large grinning person shoves a drippy spoon of orange goop under their noses and says things like "Num, num . . . open the tunnel . . . here comes the choo-choo." That may also explain the drop in recent years in passenger train traffic. No wonder so many kids suffer from PTVS: Post-Traumatic Vegetable Syndrome. Children all over the world are burying their pain in napkins, under the meatloaf, and in Rover's bowl.

As moms, our only consolation is that this veggie rejection has been going on for centuries. Mothers from ancient times probably struggled to hide Egyptian leeks in their stews. Vegetables have a long history as a rejected food group. With so many children refusing to eat their veggies, it stands to reason that another use had to be found for them. While no documented proof exists, we suspect this is where the first Halloween veggie lanterns came from. The actual facts tell another tale.

The first lanterns made from vegetables were likely hollowed-out turnips. Some historical evidence points to poor early Europeans, beginning possibly in Ireland, carving out turnips and placing candles or embers in them to use as lanterns. This tradition has been overshadowed by their symbolic use on Halloween thanks to an old Irish fable, told and retold through the generations to teach a moral. It was the legend of Jack O'Lantern.

Stingy Jack, a cranky, miserable old drunk who enjoyed playing tricks, was visited one day by the Devil who came to claim his soul. But Jack had a trick up his sleeve. He asked the Devil to climb an apple tree and get him one last apple before he had to leave earth forever. The Devil agreed, but when he did,

Stingy Old Jack placed crosses around the tree so the Devil couldn't climb down. With the Devil stuck in the tree, Jack made him promise that he would not die yet, and when he finally did, the Devil would not get his soul.

Many years later, Jack died, but because of the selfish life he'd led on earth, there was no place in heaven for him, so he was turned away. At the gates of hell, the Devil reminded him of his promise and he also turned Jack away. Jack had no place to go. Forced to wander forever between heaven and hell, Jack asked the Devil how he'd find his way with no light. In response, the Devil tossed him an ember, which Jack caught in a hollowed-out turnip. From then on, Jack roamed the earth, searching for a resting place, his turnip lantern lighting the way.

The moral is, a life lived in selfishness is a life without light.

That fable inspired the Irish tradition of hollowing out turnips, rutabagas, gourds, potatoes, and beets on All Hallows' Eve and placing a light in them to drive away the darkness of Stingy Jack and keep away such an evil spirit. Irish immigrants brought this tradition with them to America, quickly discovering that a plant in the New World was bigger and easier to carve, and pumpkins soon became the new jack-o'-lanterns.

Fables, such as this, have long been used for teaching moral and spiritual lessons. In the Bible, Jesus used parables to teach significant truths. He was a master storyteller who knew the power of a good illustration. Perhaps you remember a story Jesus told about a man who died and, finding himself in Hades, begged God to send a message back to his brothers urging them to repent so they might not find themselves in his torment one day (Luke 16:19-31) Fables, stories, and parables, though they don't always stick to reality, can make a lasting impression on those who hear them. As parents, we can employ that same tool to teach our children, even with a jack-o'-lantern.

Creatively sharing the fable of the carved pumpkin can teach some important lessons. Consider using a Halloween lantern to bring to life some amazing truths from God's Word. We've included some devotional ideas to get you started. Jack-o'-lanterns aren't anything we need to fear. If doubts start to creep in, just remember how Jesus himself taught with fables and say to yourself, "Vegetables are not evil."

TIPS FOR PUMPKIN CARVING

Devotional Ideas

🍁 Be like a Halloween pumpkin: a source of light on a dark night. As your family transforms a pumpkin into a decorative lantern, use the process to teach how we ourselves can be a better light source.

• Cutting open the top: Have the mind of Christ to think and act as He would (1 Corinthians 2:16).

• Cleaning out the seeds: Confess your sins so God can clean them out (1 John 1:9).

• Carving new eyes: Instead of looking for the faults of others, use your eyes to examine your own faults first (Matthew 7:3-5).

• Carving a nose: Don't be a proud person with your nose in the air or you will be the cause of many arguments (Proverbs 13:10).

• Carving ears: Listen to gain knowledge and tune your ears to wisdom from others (Proverbs 23:12).

• Carving a mouth: Let your words be sweet so that they will bless others (Proverbs 16:24).

• Lighting the candle: When you try to think, act, see, listen, and speak as Christ, then "your whole body is full of light, and no part of it dark, [and] it will be completely lighted, as when the light of a lamp shines on you." (Luke 11:36).

- You can give this devotion to your family using a ready-made pumpkin that you prepare beforehand. Just replace all of the cutouts and remove them one by one at the appropriate time in your presentation. You could even draw the face on with a permanent marker instead of cutting it out.

🍂 Use the carving process to share the gospel.

- Cut the pumpkin open and reveal the mess inside: No matter how our life looks on the outside, our life is really a mess and hopeless without God because of our sin (Romans 3:23).
- Turn the pumpkin upside down and try to shake out the mess: We can't get rid of our own sin. Just as a pumpkin will rot and be left useless as it is, left with our sin, we will also face ruin (Romans 6:23).
- The pumpkin is helpless to take its own mess away and needs our help: We are helpless to take our sin away and we need help too (Romans 5:6, 8).
- Remove the seeds and slime from the inside of the pumpkin: God sent Jesus to do what we couldn't, take away our sins (Romans 10:9).
- Show the clean and empty pumpkin: Once the mess has been taken away, a new space has been created for something better (Ephesians 4:22-32).
- Cut a joyful face in the pumpkin: Joy is one of the first things that God uses to fill that empty space (Romans 15:13).
- Place a candle inside the pumpkin and light it: Now our lives are a place where God lives, and when we obey Him, the light of His goodness shines through us (John 8:12).

- Set the newly carved pumpkin next to an uncarved one: When we trust Jesus to take away our sins, He makes us into a whole new creature, full of joy and light (2 Corinthians 5:17).
- Set your pumpkin out for all to see, but as you do, tell your children that the pumpkin will eventually rot and perish: Those with the real light of Christ, though, will never perish, because we have eternal life (John 3:16).

Tips for Carving

🍁 Materials include:
- Something to cover your work surface (newspapers work well).
- A number of pumpkins: If your children are very young, you may want to have one pumpkin that you all help with together. For older children, they may each want their own pumpkin to carve.
- A permanent marker for drawing lines before cutting.
- A knife, box cutter, or for younger children, a safety knife.
- A trash can or plastic bag for easy cleanup.
- A wet washrag and paper towels to clean your hands as you work.
- Small tea lights or other type of candles.
- Matches or a lighter.
- A camera.
- A Bible or cards with devotional verses.

🍁 Have drinks available.

🍁 Unplug the phone.

🍁 If you like, explain the process beforehand. Let children know that they will have to be patient; carving may take longer than they think.

❀ Make the rules very clear about handling the knives you have set out.

❀ If you are working with young children and you are letting each carve their own pumpkin, it is best to have one adult assigned to help each child.

❀ You may want to hand out aprons to protect clothes, and if possible carve outside or in the garage.

❀ If you are afraid that your young ones will lose interest in the process or in the devotional, carve the pumpkin and later come back to teach the devotional. Set aside some of the slimy seeds in the refrigerator to use.

❀ When the pumpkin is finished, be sure to choose a cool location out of direct sunlight, telling kids that it will eventually rot and have to be thrown out. Even this, though, is an opportunity to teach them that, unlike the pumpkin, we will never be thrown out. With the light of Christ in us, we have eternal life (John 3:16).

MOVIES, MEMORIES, & MONSTERS

Kim and Pam Go Hollywood

America has a love affair with the movies, and so do Pam and I. For me it started on a family outing in the backseat of my parents' station wagon. After slipping into our pajamas and helping mom fill a grocery bag full of popcorn, our family was off to the drive-in theatre. There, before my very eyes, unforgettable characters three stories tall were indelibly stamped into my memory. For days and even weeks afterward, I became my favorite character. For a time, my dreams and even my future plans were based on the two-hour movie plot that came through the mono speaker hanging from my dad's car window.

Movies are like that for many of us. Whether we plan it or not, often it is more than mere entertainment. Subtly or not so subtly, movies can change the way we think, the way we view the world, even the way we behave. Pam tells how *Jaws* forever changed her life.

I didn't generally watch scary movies, but somehow *Jaws* slipped through the cracks. Weeks after watching that great white monster terrorize a community, my family went water skiing at Lake Ransom Canyon, our favorite summer getaway. I loved to ski, but this time as Dad offered for me to go first, I graciously declined and stayed in the boat. After everyone had skied and Dad said that it was my turn, I still passed. So out of character for my usual eager enthusiasm, Dad asked me why I wouldn't ski. I said I just wasn't in the mood, but the truth was, I was in sheer panic. What was out there below the surface? I could hear the music in my head . . . du-du, du-du . . . It was going to get me! I was sure that I didn't have a chance since I had cut my leg shaving that morning. Any evil creature would be drawn by my dot of blood and I'd be a goner. At that moment, I doubted I would ever ski again. Eventually of course, I did, but not without a new sense of uncertainty and fear I hadn't experienced before.

Sometimes the powerful change movies inspire is a good thing. How many little girls have seen themselves as princesses because of Cinderella? How many boys have aspired to be someone's hero because of Superman?

There is just something about the power of storytelling combined with visual images that resonates long after the lights come up. Even one line in a movie can bring it all back as if we had just seen it yesterday.

"Life is like a box of _____."

"The name is Bond, _____."

"Lions and tigers and _____, oh my."

"May the _____ be with you."

"Go ahead, make my ____."

"Every time a bell rings an _____ gets his _____."

Even now when a bell rings, many of us think about Clarence. *It's a Wonderful Life* is a movie we watch in the Wier family only at Christmastime, along with *Rudolf the Red-Nosed Reindeer, Miracle on 34th Street, A Charlie Brown Christmas,* and *The Little Drummer Boy.* Watching these movies together as a family has become an important part of our holiday tradition.

Together they sum up what the season means to us. It's about hope, fun, faith, and the greatest gift of all time. We could watch them in July, but the true impact would be lost out of season.

The same is true for our Easter staples. We love reliving the Passover story of the Exodus and the parting of the Red Sea in *The Ten Commandments.* Can you imagine getting to heaven and finding that Moses doesn't really look like Charlton Heston? Our family also loves the film, *Jesus.* These two movies give our family just one more way to celebrate God's incredible love for us during the Easter season.

There is great potential to use movies to make your Halloween celebration more meaningful, as well. There are many movies that tell the stories of faith heroes. Other films, while not all box office hits, definitely are worth considering for the stories of the heroes who risked everything for their faith in Jesus Christ. Whether you have very young children, elementary age kids, or teenagers, these quality videos could become your family's seasonal must-sees.

Another twist is to have a movie night that focuses on specific character qualities of those heroes worth emulating, or a particular Christian theme or quality fantasy movie that captures the fun of the season. You can even use movies based on fictional characters to teach redeeming moral lessons.

A movie night with a redemption theme is a wonderful opportunity for celebration. By establishing this kind of a movie night during the Halloween season, kids will have fun being introduced—maybe for the first time—to these unique characters and faith heroes. Along with the titles, we've suggested some creative ways to turn an ordinary movie night into a memorable holiday event.

And don't be surprised if after experiencing your movie night, your family makes this a traditional part of every Halloween season.

TIPS FOR A SEASONAL MOVIE NIGHT
Movies for All Ages

❧ While there are some wonderful videos that present the lives of heroes of the faith from different periods in history, some videos are more suitable for younger or older ages. Be sure to preview anything you aren't sure about and consider attention spans and interest levels.

- *VeggieTales* (Ages 2-10) Titles that retell the story of Old Testament heroes—animated entertainment: *Rack, Shack and Benny; Dave and the Giant Pickle; Joshua and the Big Wall; Esther: The Girl Who Became Queen; Jonah the Movie.* (Another VeggieTales title you might consider for Halloween is *Where's God When I'm Scared?*)

- *StoryKeepers* (Ages 6-12) Videos distributed by Zondervan that reenact circumstances of early church persecution—animated entertainment: *Breakout!; Catacomb Rescue; Ready, Aim, Fire; Roar in the Night; Captured; Trapped*

- **Children's Heroes from Christian History Video Series** (Ages 5-10) Video stories about heroes of faith from various periods of church history, still pictures narrated in story form. Volumes One, Two, and Three

- *Present Time Video Series* (Ages 8-14) Movies of current-day kids who get to use a time machine to meet heroes of the faith—not animated. Titles include: *The Adventure Begins; The Fiery Stranger; The Lost Prophet*

- Non-Series Videos: **Stephen's Test of Faith** (Ages 8 & up) The life of the first New Testament martyr.

❧ Movies for Preteen to Adult

- **Classics Movies of Faith Heroes**: *Spartacus; Ben Hur; The Robe*

- **Pre-Twentieth-Century Faith Heroes** (Distributed by Vision Video): *Paul, the Emissary; Martin Luther; Candle in the Dark, The Story of William Carey; John Hus*
- **Twentieth-Century Faith Heroes** (Distributed by Vision Video): *Bonhoeffer, Agent of Grace; China Cry: The True Story of Nora Lam; Going Home: The Journey of Kim Jones* (teen killed in 1999 in Texas Baptist church shooting)
- **Missionary Story Videos** (Distributed by Vision Video) *First Fruits: Zinzendorf and the Moravians; Beyond the Next Mountain,* about reaching the Hmar tribe.
- **The Story of Eric Liddell**—There are two great resources that work well together to tell Eric Liddell's story. First watch *Chariots of Fire,* and then follow it up with the compelling documentary feature that gives the rest of the story of Liddell's fascinating life as a missionary. The documentary title is *The Story of Eric Liddell: An Olympic Gold Medalist's Lifelong Race to Spread the Gospel* (also available through Vision Video). There is also a review and discussion questions of *Chariots of Fire* in the book *Movie Nights,* published by Focus on the Family.
- **Documentary-Style Videos** (Distributed by Vision Video) *Through Gates of Splendor* (The Jim and Elisabeth Elliot story)
- **Documentaries from The Voice of the Martyrs** (Distributed by Vision Video) *The Martyr's Cry* (three true life stories); *Faith Under Fire* (interviews with Christians who face persecution head-on)

To locate movies: We recommend both Focus on the Family (family.org) and Vision Video (visionvideo.com) as reliable sources. They have many other movies and audio titles not mentioned here that are also suitable for Halloween.

Some other ideas might be Disney's *Prince of Egypt* for ages 10 and up; or for teens, *Ever After, A Knight's Tale, Galaxy Quest,* or *Unbreakable*. Parents should preview the films beforehand and be aware that each has a few unsavory elements (including an implied sex scene between the leads in *A Knight's Tale*). See the book *Movie Nights* for specifics and recommended discussion questions for these and other family films.

Making It an Event

- 🍁 Create an atmosphere that matches the time period of the movie. For example, your teens would love a Toga Movie Night if you choose to watch *Spartacus* or *Ben Hur.* (Toga Movie Night also makes a fun teen outreach during the Halloween season. Show the movie and challenge them with the gospel. Additional details are in the tips for the Fill-in-the-Gap Party.)

- 🍁 If you are really creative, decorate the room to match the theme. For example, an Olympic theme for *Chariots of Fire.*

- 🍁 Serve food that sets the mood. For example, serve veggie snacks (French fries count) if you are going to watch a VeggieTales movie or Chinese takeout if you are watching *China Cry.*

- 🍁 With young children, make it a night to cuddle.

- 🍁 Plan an intermission and serve ice cream sundaes.

- 🍁 Be sure to save time at the end of the movie to talk. "What do you think was that person's strongest character trait?" "How hard do you think it was for them to make the right choices?" "What about that person would you like to imitate?" "Do you ever feel like that person did?" "How has your own faith been tested this week?"

🍁 However you choose to plan your Halloween season movie night, enjoy being together and have fun!

UNDERGROUND CHURCH PARTY

Pam Brings Down the House

S ome people think there is a fine art to throwing a memorable party. I discovered that memorable isn't always the best aim.

During my college years, a friend and I wanted to come up with the most creative dinner party our buddies had ever attended. The plan was to invite our guests to have dinner at a secret location. To solve the mystery, they would go on a scavenger hunt that would eventually lead them to their final destination—my parents' house. Mom and Dad were going out of town and gave permission for us to play hostesses in their absence.

We just knew this would be the most unforgettable party our friends had ever attended. Everyone was excited as the clues were passed out and the adventure began. While our guests were trying to find their way to the dinner, Betsy and I started the cooking. We were just giddy with our own cleverness.

The first guest, Doug, arrived just as Betsy was heating the oil for our homemade French fries. Doug began entertaining us with the adventures he encountered following our intricate clues. Listening intently to his story, we forgot all about the pan on the stove—that is, until it took off into orbit. Did you know that a pan of superheated grease is combustible? My first instinct was to locate the box of baking soda and throw it on the fire, but those cabinets were already burning. So I grabbed a nearby hand towel and tossed it on the flames—adding more fuel. Within seconds the stove area was a towering inferno that was punctuated with even more drama when the electricity blew. Doug told Betsy to call 911, but I protested.

"People will know there was a fire if you call!"

Ignoring me, Betsy made the call. Not willing to let my parents' house go without a fight, I ran to look for a blanket to smother the fire. Knowing that precious seconds could make all the difference, I found myself debating which blanket to choose. Grandmothers quilt? No. Mom's afghan? No way! I spied the old electric blanket. Perfect. We didn't have electricity anymore anyway. Only sheer adrenaline could have accounted for our success in beating out the blaze with that poor blanket.

With the flames extinguished and the cabinets smoldering, we stood in silence listening to the sirens wail ever nearer. At least the party would be easy for our friends to find. All they'd have to do was look for the house with smoke billowing from the windows. And that's just what many people did. In fact, the entire neighborhood turned out. It was the most memorable block party we'd had in years.

I've learned much about throwing parties these past 20 years, including the value of catering and of simple creativity. A memorable party doesn't have to wow your guests with elaborate decorations or costly extras. What most people, including children, remember about a party is whether there's a fire. Just kidding. It's whether they felt welcomed, were with good friends, and had a good time.

Parties that commemorate certain events or seasons are especially memorable. Who doesn't love attending a Christmas or a birthday party? It's an occasion to celebrate an important something or someone. They are events that are talked about for days and sometimes even weeks to come.

Why not add Halloween to that category? Not in the usual way, but with a party that celebrates the history and adventure of the early church heroes.

An Underground Church Party is full of action and fun as kids discover the risks that people around the world can face when they choose to follow Christ. The party can include games, dressing up, easy snacks, and a devotional, and it can help kids grow a real heart for believers around the world.

We have hosted a party like this for our elementary-aged children and their friends, and they talked about it for weeks afterward. You don't have to be a master entertainer to host an Underground Church Party for 8-12-year-olds. Because of its unique theme, it does require planning and some advance prepa ration, but absolutely no special skill or extravagant expense With just a willing heart and a spirit for fun, you can throw the best Halloween party in town.

TIPS FOR HOSTING AN UNDERGROUND CHURCH PARTY
Planning

 What persecuted group of people will your guests be
role-playing? You can choose a time in the past or
present. For example, in present-day China it is illegal
to meet in unauthorized churches. You could hold
your party in Russia in the 1920s, or Rome in A.D.
150. If you are looking for inspiration, visit Voice
of the Martyrs' Web site (www.persecution.com) or
their kids' Web site (www.linkingup.com), or check
out any book on martyrs from the library (e.g., *Foxe's
Book of Martyrs*).

 If you choose a time period that's distinctive in dress,
allow costumes.

❧ To have a successful Underground Church Party you need about 20 guests. However, more would only make the event more interesting.

❧ Send invitations at least two weeks in advance so that you have time to receive RSVP responses and attendees have time to put together costumes. Be sure to check your church and community calendar for conflicts before you choose your date.

❧ Design your invitations on the computer to match the theme and time period of your party.

❧ While this is not a complicated party, it does take some advance preparation and organization.

❧ It will also require a few extra adults or teens to assist you at the event. Consider recruiting some other parents to cohost with you.

❧ Because this party works well with larger numbers, you might consider hosting it through your church and using the fellowship hall.

Preparing

Secretly assign each child to be one of the following groups: an established church member, a new Christian convert, or a member of the secret police. Designate one person to be the pastor. Each of the players will receive a packet with different documents when they arrive, but no one will know who's who until the game is underway.

Packet for Church Members:

❧ Select a secret meeting location for each of the groups. If there are three groups you will need three separate locations.

❧ Each group member must be given written directions to the meeting location.

❧ Instead of drawing a map, you will give them clues and
landmarks to navigate by.

For example, if this event were to be held in my
house and yard I would plan on posting signs in different rooms and locations that rename the areas. In my
dining room I might hang a sign that says "Butcher
Shop." The living room might be labeled "Cobblers."
Do this for every room and even areas of the yard.
Also post "street signs" that they can use for directions. Since you will not want to hang these signs
until the day of the event, draw your own map of
your house and label it so that you can prepare the
directions for each guest's secret packet. Then save
the map to use as a guide for hanging signs on the
day of the party.

❧ Write directions that will lead each group on a round-
about path to find their safe meeting house. Since they
will not have a map, they will have to stop at every
location you designate. (At each of these locations,
place a stamp on their secret papers to show they
have correctly followed the directions.)

❧ Once you have a master copy of the directions to each
safe house, make enough copies for each member of
that secret group.

❧ Choose a secret password question for each group that
will also be included in church member packets. An
example would be "Is it supposed to rain tonight?"

❧ Choose a secret response to the password that each
group will use to identify one another. An example
would be "No, but the moon is very bright."

❧ The last item for the church member packets will be an
index card with the words "ID Card" and a new name

for that guest that comes from the culture you are role-playing.

🍁 Also in each packet will be the role that guest will play: Secret Underground Church Member.

🍁 The final completed packet for a church member will include: a Role Card telling what part they will play in the game; one set of directions to a secret church meeting house; password question and answer for that house's members; and ID Card.

Packet for Underground Church Pastor:

🍁 This packet will include everything that the church member gets, except his Role Card will say "Church Pastor" and he will receive a photocopy of one page of New Testament scripture.

Packet for New Christians looking for a church:

🍁 This packet will include a Role Card telling their part and an ID Card. They will not have directions or passwords. These people must try to be accepted by the group by convincing them they are sincere new converts.

Packet for Secret Police:

🍁 Their packet will contain an ID Card that designates them as police.

🍁 A fake ID that has a name but does not say "Police" that they will use to try to infiltrate the church members.

🍁 The police also do not get a password or directions and must try to infiltrate the groups by pretending to be new Christians looking for an underground church.

🍁 All of the packets will look exactly alike on the outside. No one will know when you hand them out who is who. Only by exchanging passwords will they be able to identify their group and work together to make it to the safe meeting house.

The Game

- ❦ When guests arrive they all meet in one room.
- ❦ When everyone is there, explain the setting. This is best done with a story. For instance, "It's 1920. This is Russia and Christians are hated by the government . . ."
- ❦ Explain that to worship, they must meet secretly. If they openly worship they will be arrested and put in jail.
- ❦ Tell them how many different safe houses are to be part of your event. For example, if you have 25 kids, you should have four secret safe houses with four church members traveling to each. There will be five new believers looking for safe meeting houses to join and four secret police posing as new believers.
- ❦ Explain that the goal of the church members is to make it to the safe house to meet, worship, memorize the scripture the pastor has, and break up before being caught by the secret police who will be looking for them.
- ❦ Announce that the pastor(s) will lead the worship meeting only when at least three of the church members arrive (or more depending on the number in each group—aim for half the members) and cannot dismiss the group for 10 minutes once the majority has arrived and worship begins.
- ❦ Announce the number of secret police who will be trying to sneak into a group and attend the secret meeting. They must be careful who they travel with and what they say.
- ❦ If the secret police are able to join your group by pretending to be Christians, the entire group immediately goes to jail once the worship begins and the secret police arrest them.

❧ The underground group who meets for the full 10 minutes, is not infiltrated by secret police, and is able to memorize at least one verse gets a prize.

❧ Announce that any group that accepts a real new believer—even if they are caught—gets a bonus.

❧ The police who successfully infiltrate a group also win a prize.

❧ Adults represent the government and can stop anyone for an ID check to ask where they are going.

❧ Plan for the game to take about 30 minutes.

Devotional Time

❧ Let everyone identify who they played.

❧ Talk about how hard it was to operate when you didn't know who was watching.

❧ Read a true story about someone who actually lived under those circumstances. *Foxe's Book of Martyrs* or the books in the *Jesus Freaks* series are good resources for these.

❧ Ask the kids questions about what it would be like if Christians had to hide their faith in America or worry that they could be arrested for believing in Jesus.

❧ Explain that Jesus said we should all expect that people in the world would hate us because we love Him. Read John 15:18-20:

> If the world hates you, keep in mind that it hated me first. If you belonged to the world, it would love you as its own. As it is, you do not belong to the world, but I have chosen you out of the world. That is why the world hates you. Remember the words I spoke to

you: "No servant is greater than his master." If they persecuted me, they will persecute you also. If they obeyed my teaching, they will obey yours also.

🍁 Remind them that we can be grateful to be in America where we can worship openly, but we can also pray for those around the world who suffer for believing in Jesus.

🍁 Challenge them to share what they know about Jesus with their friends because not everyone has the same privilege and we should not waste it.

🍁 Pray for them as a group to stand firm in their faith and to share what they know.

Food and Prizes

🍁 Either have snacks set out as all the groups come in and before devotional time, or have them available afterward. Keep it simple. Store-bought cookies and chips are usually a hit.

🍁 Hand out prizes won during the game as people are getting ready to leave: a small toy or a candy bar. A dollar store is a good resource for inexpensive prizes.

Communicating
the Message

Rejoice with me;
I have found my lost sheep.
—LUKE 15:6

DOORS OF OPPORTUNITY

Pam Almost Conquers the World

I was 17 years old, and like most soon-to-be high school graduates, I was ready to see my hometown in my rearview mirror. Growing up in Lubbock, Texas, had been fine, but I was ready for a change. I wanted to break out of my mold, make new friends, and conquer the world. For me, new opportunities could only be found on the horizon.

I shared my plans to leave Lubbock with my parents, who then shared their plan with me. In unison they announced, "We'll pay for you to attend Texas Tech here in Lubbock or Texas Tech here in Lubbock." That was a tough choice. Stay in Lubbock, with Mom and Dad picking up the tab, or see Lubbock from my rearview mirror penniless. I decided to conquer the world, starting in Lubbock. Besides, living on the Texas Tech campus was totally different than living in Lubbock, and I'd also have my friend Reneta to share the adventure.

Together, we made plans to experience dorm life as roommates. I hardly remembered that I was in Lubbock at all as we picked out matching comforters and room decorations. That's when Reneta dropped the bomb. She announced that she planned to join a sorority and would be participating in "rush." She was actually excited about the prospect of spending a week visiting different "invitation-only" parties as part of the sorority selection process. I couldn't have been more shocked. We hadn't discussed conquering sororities together.

"Why would you do that?" I asked in my best "good girl" voice. "Sororities are all so wild." (I had seen *Animal House*.) But Reneta had made up her mind. She wanted to explore all of her opportunities, even sorority life.

At home, I shared with my mom how my friend had lost her mind. I was shocked again at the advice my mother gave me: "If I could do one thing about my college years over again, Pam, I would have joined a social sorority." I was so surprised to get that perspective from "Ms. Valedictorian." *She* was the one who always stressed focusing on education. I was comfortable with that. But she continued, "Pam, college is about learning to have a balanced life. That doesn't just include studying and making good grades. Relationships are important, and so is a healthy social life."

The next week I signed up for rush with Reneta. I still wasn't sure if I wanted to join a sorority, but I would attend the parties and explore my opportunities, too. I could decide later if I wanted to make a commitment, though I was doubtful I would. My rush counselor had doubts too, when day after day I asked, "Now, how do I drop out if I decide that I don't want to do this?"

The entire process was an emotional roller coaster. I liked the prospect of making so many new friends, belonging to a group, and feeling wanted. Yet I cringed at the thought of being rejected. Each time I expressed official interest in a sorority, I knew I was taking a risk that they might not choose me. I didn't care what my mom said. I'd rather be socially stunted than out-right rejected. That was a stressful week, but I stuck it out because I was beginning to like the girls I had met. From the very first time a sorority door was opened and I was welcomed in, it was as if the whole group had been waiting for me to arrive.

Everyone wanted to be my new best friend! As a rushee, they made me feel like it was "all about me."

After five whirlwind days, I had to choose my sorority. I had met some wonderful girls whom I wanted the opportunity to know better. So I chose. Then I waited. For 24 hours, suspense gave way to dread as I imagined what it would be like when they said "No, thanks. We want someone else."

I'll never forget finally going to the post office the next day and retrieving my sorority card. With trembling hands, I broke the seal and opened the envelope. I felt dizzy as I read, "You are invited to become a Kappa Kappa Gamma. . . . Meet us at the fountain."

I was wanted! Just knowing that gave me wings, and I flew through a sea of other pledges toward "my group." As I approached the Kappas who had given me such validation, I heard cheers all around me. The sincerity with which I was welcomed is something I will never forget. They didn't just want me. They really truly wanted me.

The relationship seeds that were planted at that very first rush party grew as I spent time with my new Kappa Sisters. It was just the first step toward the fostering of lasting relationships that were far more significant than just a mere social life. God used my welcome to Kappa as His invitation for me to invest in others and to share His love with them. And it all began with just that one open door.

Since then, I have asked God to allow me to be the one with the open-door policy. Part of my husband, Jerry's, and my ministry with Campus Crusade in the past has been to welcome college students anytime day or night to show them they were "wanted." Significant relationships followed, and we saw God open hearts simply because we were willing to first open our door. It was a tried-and-true way to reach out and have a lasting influence in the lives of the students and our way of fulfilling God's call.

> Devote yourselves to prayer, keeping alert in it with an
> attitude of thanksgiving; praying at the same time for us as
> well, that God will open up to us a door for the word, so
> that we may speak forth the mystery of Christ. (Colossians
> 4:2-3, NASB)

Every one of us has been called to look for open doors to
share the love of Christ and to make the most of every opportunity, even with outsiders—sometimes known as our neighbors. Yet with our busy lives and a long list of church
commitments, often finding time to share Christ with our
neighbors is a challenge.

What if God would arrange for your neighbors to knock on
your door—and not just one neighbor, but the entire neighborhood—in just one night? Would you be willing to open your
door for the chance to "make the most of the opportunity"?
Well, get ready, because on October 31, God will be sending
them your way! Of course, you might not recognize them
because they could be dressed in superhero costumes and car-
rying buckets of candy, but they *will* be knocking on your door.
The only question is how best to make the most of that opportunity. We have a few suggestions.

Take a look at the list of tips for receiving trick-or-treaters.
When you take the first step of initiating a friendship by sincerely
welcoming those whom God brings your way, you open the door
for God to work through your hospitality. When you make your
neighbors feel wanted, *truly* wanted, their response might surprise you.

Christ initiated a relationship with us first, and the conse-
quences were powerful. When we follow that example and
engage those around us with a sincere hand of friendship, we
can expect positive results as well.

Tips for Welcoming Trick-or-Treaters

Preparing for Visitors

🍁 Whether your family participates in trick-or-treating or not, have a lights-on policy. Notes that ask your neighbors not to knock because you don't "do" Halloween, no matter how kindly worded, leave others feeling judged.

🍁 The treats you give out say a great deal about your family to the kids who knock on your door. Just like we used to do, they all go home and talk about who offered the best stuff. It is part of the whole experience, like trading candy with your brothers and sisters to get what you really want. When deciding what treats you will give out, consider these options:

- Be known as a generous giver. Give the best candy bars on the block, not the least you can get away with. It will make more of an impression than you can imagine.

- If you want to offer a spiritual treat, make sure it is accompanied by a sweet treat. The last thing you want is to give something spiritual and have the first response be disappointment.

- One way to give something spiritual along with something sweet is to use your computer to make candy-bar wrappers with a Bible message. Design and print a message on colorful paper, wrap the candy around the normal wrapper, and secure it with tape or a glue stick. A sample message might be: "Taste and see that the Lord is good" (Psalm 34:8); or "How sweet are [God's] words to my taste, sweeter than honey to my mouth!" (Psalm 119:103).

- If you have many trick-or-treaters who are not from your neighborhood, you may not have the opportunity to follow up by fostering a personal relationship. In this case, you may want to give out children's gospel tracts.
- If your budget allows, one great giveaway is Focus on the Family's *Adventures in Odyssey* audio tapes. You can often find them at your local Christian bookstore packaged as single tapes at a low promotional price.

🍁 As you fill your jars with candy and turn on the lights, take time to pray as a family for all those who will come to your door. Ask God to give you just the right words for each person you greet and to use the night to prepare the way for building relationships in which you can share His love.

🍁 Get into the spirit of the celebration. Greet your visitors dressed in costume, even if it is just a silly hat or a painted-on mustache.

🍁 Lock up any pets that might cause problems.

Making the Most of Opportunities with Children

🍁 Be outside on the porch, if possible.

🍁 Greet the kids with words that let them know they are truly welcome. For example, say, "We've been waiting for you," or, "We're so glad you came to our house."

🍁 Ask their names, and try to make a mental note to remember them in the future.

🍁 Show interest by asking about their costumes.

🍁 If you are wearing a costume, use opportunities to talk about it as they arise. Remember, though, that you are there to build relationships, not to preach or try to change their views of Halloween.

Making the Most of Opportunities with Parents

❧ If parents are not coming to the door, bring your candy to them.

❧ Weather permitting, have a treat for parents as well.

  • If it is cold, have coffee and tea in paper cups.

  • If it's warm, offer bottled water from an ice chest.

  • Have a bowl of mints.

❧ Introduce yourself to the parents, and ask where they live.

❧ If you know anything at all about them (where they work, what kind of dog they have, etc.), show interest, but keep it brief, as kids will be anxious to get to the next house.

❧ Before parting, let them know how pleased you were to meet them and express interest in seeing them again.

Keeping the Door Open

❧ If your memory needs a little help, make a note of the names of the neighbors you meet.

❧ Begin to pray for those families by name.

❧ Ask God to give you natural opportunities to build on your Halloween introductions.

❧ Watch to see where God is working.

❧ Slow down and take advantage of little opportunities. When you see a neighbor mowing the lawn or walking the dog, take a few minutes and stop to say hello.

❧ Invite a mom over for coffee, or ask a dad for a helping hand with a home project.

❧ If there are children your kids could get to know, call and invite them over to play, and tell them they can bring their parents, too!

❧ Be prepared! If you sincerely want to reach out to others with the love of God in your own neighborhood, God will faithfully give you many opportunities.

FEAR-NOT PARTY

Kim's Transylvania Terror

I will never forget the night I saw my first werewolf. I was six years old, and I was sharing the recliner with my cousin. It was the first time I had been allowed to watch *Dark Shadows* with the big kids. I don't recall the plot of the only episode I ever watched, but I do remember the scene that started my lifelong battle against werewolves.

Picture with me a dark night: a sky void of stars, made even more ominous by the black trailing clouds that obscured a full moon. In the pasture below, a girl walks alone, unaware of the danger that surrounds her, but we in the television audience know it's coming. The music swells. An owl hoots with intensity. She is startled. None of us dares to breathe. Something is about to happen.

I gripped my cousin tightly with one hand, burying my face in her sleeve. With the other hand, I had a death grip on the arm of the recliner. I couldn't see, but I *could* hear the approaching danger. The music grew louder. My palms began to sweat. I dared a peek through my fingers. Something was moving in the distance on the black-and-white TV screen. It was coming. It was coming. It was . . . A scream pierced the silence, but it wasn't coming from the television. It was coming from me. Something hairy had touched my hand, and I panicked, setting off a chain reaction. Everyone in the room began to scream.

After what seemed like eternity, the lights came on in the room. My heart was pounding, and I was crying. The room was in chaos. That's when we saw it. My "werewolf" dog, Ginger, had brushed by my hand and was now cowering in the corner. She soon recovered, but I never did. From that moment on, the dark became my enemy, and fear was my constant companion.

My parents did all the right things. They assured me that vampires and werewolves were imaginary, just like munchkins, hobbits, and elves. However, if it turned out they were wrong, a munchkin wasn't going to suck my blood and turn me into the walking dead! Like the cowardly lion in *The Wizard of Oz*, I would say to myself, "I don't believe in spooks. I don't believe in spooks. I *do* believe in spooks. I do, I do, I do!" I decided I would believe—just to be on the safe side—and I did for years. Every night, I slept with the covers over my neck to guard against fangs.

My sister, Tammi, was oblivious to the lurking danger. Two years older than I, she often let me sleep in her room. There I felt safe, although I never understood what kept the monsters out of her space. Was it her psychedelic strobe light? The endless repetition of "I Shot the Sheriff" on her record player?

Escaping to Tammi's room was only a temporary solution. Inevitably, I would be sent packing, back to my own room to face my fears alone. Night after night, year after year, I fought a lonely battle that only halted when the sun came up. By the time I was a teen, I knew, intellectually, there were no such things, but I was afraid to say it out loud, scared they'd hunt me down. I clung to my fear for protection. As an adult, I only shed my fear of monsters; the fear of darkness remained. When the sun went down, the panic could be paralyzing. I knew it was unreasonable. What I didn't know was how to overcome it.

Desperate to finally be rid of the irrational fear, I began to look up verses in the Bible that addressed it. The first one I read I knew God had written just for me. God had said to Kim, "Do not be afraid of sudden fear nor of the onslaught of the wicked when it comes; for the LORD will be your confidence and will keep your foot from being caught" (Proverbs 3:25-26, NASB).

I memorized those promises that very day. Over the following three weeks as I lay in bed, afraid of what I could not see, I went over and over those verses, reminding myself that "it is impossible for God to lie" (Hebrews 6:18).

As I stored God's truth in my heart, a miracle happened. The darkness was driven out. After 20 years of torment, I no longer feared the night. In fact, the situation had changed to be the extreme opposite. In just three weeks, I couldn't sleep if there were lights on in the house. When I discovered the "LORD [as my] confidence," "sudden fear" lost its hold over my heart and mind.

As a parent, I have done everything I can to minimize my children's struggle with fear—but kids will be kids. Even if we prevent them from watching scary programs, assure them that God is with them, and try to take the mystery out of the dark, something will eventually come along to create fear. It is a natural response to the unknown. The best way to conquer it is with a supernatural solution that confronts mystery with truth.

Over and over again in the Scriptures, God tells His people to "fear not," and almost every time, it is given as an encouragement to help them face the unknown. How do we know that we can conquer fear? Because God "has not given us a spirit of fear, but of power and of love and of a sound mind" (2 Timothy 1:7, NKJV). God Himself is not a God of fear, and He doesn't want His children to be held captive by it either. He gives His people the courage and strength to face any foe with Him by their side.

Isn't that what Halloween is about for the Christian? It is a season of commemorating ordinary people who did not "fear those who kill the body but are unable to kill the soul; but rather fear[ed] Him who is able to destroy both soul and body in hell" (Matthew 10:28, NASB).

The Fear-Not Halloween Party is just one creative way to help your elementary-aged children realize that our God is not the God of fear, and that no matter what comes, the "Lord will be [their] confidence." It is a welcome message for those who belong to Christ—or for those who have never met Jesus Christ, making it a great outreach.

What is a party, though, without fun and games? When my family hosts this celebration, it is an outside event with s'mores, a costume parade, Romans-versus-Christian Flashlight Tag, and a "scary" story around the campfire. While the whole party is fun, we have found that it is the story that makes the biggest impression, because it is always the tale of someone who faced the greatest unknown and conquered his fear. It is the story of one of the heroes of the faith from the era of the church's early persecution. All eyes will be on you as you take them back in time to discover how one person conquered real evil and made an amazing difference in God's kingdom.

The Fear-Not Halloween Party is not an *alternative* to a Halloween event. Instead, it celebrates the very heart of the season by rejoicing in God's goodness and communicating the message that faith drives out fear.

TIPS FOR HOSTING A FEAR-NOT PARTY
Planning
❀ Brainstorm with your kids the children to invite. Because your focus is on outreach, aim for diversity in backgrounds. Your children have many friends and acquaintances at school, on sports teams, and through other extracurricular activities who could be invited. This event works great for any number of kids.

🍁 Design an invitation that includes the words *Fear-Not Halloween Party*. This communicates to both kids and parents that your party will have a healthy focus.

🍁 The invitation should include a reminder to bring a flashlight and to dress up for the costume contest, noting that non-scary costumes are appropriate.

🍁 There are many things going on in communities during the month of October so be sure that you check the calendar when choosing the date. We like hosting this on a school night since weekends get so busy, and not on Halloween night as many children will participate in trick-or-treating. Our last Fear-Not Party was on a Tuesday night from 6:30-8:00. That gave parents the chance to get home from work, but also ended early enough not to interfere with homework.

🍁 Snacks are always a big hit with kids 7 to 12. On a table outside, set out bowls of popcorn, store-bought cookies, chips and dip, a jug of lemonade, and hot chocolate. Use paper goods to make cleanup easy. Set a trash can nearby.

🍁 If local city regulations allow it, a campfire will really set the mood for the party and the devotional story. The kids will also love making s'mores over the fire. Get the wood stacked and ready before guests arrive. Don't light the fire until there is at least one adult who can attend it at all times during the party. If a fire isn't an option, use a barbeque grill or even an indoor fireplace.

🍁 Set out a tray with everything needed to make the s'mores: unwrapped chocolate squares, graham crackers, large marshmallows, and skewers or straightened clothes hangers.

🍁 Situate hay bales, lawn chairs, or picnic blankets to provide places to sit.

🍁 For safety (and for your own sanity), recruit some parental help. If possible, assign one parent to the snack table, one to the fire, and another to help you organize and carry out the games. Remember, you will be reaching out to these parents with your message as much as to their kids.

🍁 Set out extra flashlights with fresh batteries, and have sticky labels available to put names on them as kids arrive.

🍁 Hang a whistle around your neck to use for the game.

At the Party

🍁 As guests arrive, allow the kids to play in the yard, visit the snack table, and greet one another.

🍁 Once most everyone is there, blow your whistle and welcome them to your Fear-Not Halloween Party.

🍁 Explain what you will be doing and emphasize any guidelines or safety rules.

🍁 We usually start our party with Flashlight Tag, renamed Romans-versus-Christians Flashlight Tag. We start with this game because it provides a natural way to explain the real history behind Halloween. Here's how the game works:

  • Tell the following story: "After Jesus left earth to return to heaven, His followers began to spread the Good News, and the church began. Unfortunately, not everyone wanted the news spread. The Roman government wanted to stop Christians from telling others about Jesus, so they did everything they could to stop them. They hunted Christians down, arrested them, and sometimes even killed them. Christians had to learn to tell others about Christ while avoiding arrest by the Romans. For three hundred years, Rome hunted the Christians. Finally, one Roman emperor became a Christian himself, and the terrible persecution ended in Rome. However, so many faithful men and women had died that the church decided to set aside a special day to remember them. They called that special day 'All Saints' Day,' and the night before it they named 'Halloween,' or 'Eve of the Holy Ones.' That is why we have Halloween today. And in honor of its beginnings, we are going to play Romans-versus-Christians Flashlight Tag."

- The rules: In the first game, all of the kids are Christians. Three adults or teen helpers are the Romans. The Christians will get a two-minute head start. They must hide somewhere in the yard to avoid getting caught. Be sure to set clear boundaries for the game. The Romans will have flashlights, and they will search for the Christians until they find all of them. If a Roman sees a Christian and hits him with a beam of light from the flashlight, he is caught and has to turn himself in at the jail, located at the campfire (or other designated area). The game ends after a set time limit (approximately 10 minutes), or when all are caught—whichever comes first. Blow the whistle to indicate when the game ends.

- Be prepared. Kids will want to play this several times, and they will also want to volunteer to be the Romans. Each time a game ends, give a prize to the Christians who remained uncaught when time ran out. The length of your party will determine the number of rounds you can play. Reserve at least 45 minutes for other activities.

- Fun prizes can be purchased at the dollar store. We put several dollar prizes in a box and let the winners choose.

- Have the s'mores tray waiting by the fireplace or campfire for any kids who get caught. They can fix themselves a s'more while waiting for the next game to start. Keep the s'more tray available all night for kids who don't get a chance to make one while in jail.

❧ You should have time for a costume parade to allow kids to show off their costumes. A front porch works very well for this. Have everyone stand on the lawn facing the porch. If you have a portable stereo, play some upbeat music. With five kids at a time waiting in the wings, let them parade across the porch in front of the audience displaying the costume "in character." Give prizes for those who do the best impersonation. You may also decide to give prizes for creative costumes from your dollar prize box. The costume parade should not take more than 10 to 15 minutes, depending on the number of guests.

❧ After the parade, gather guests at the campfire. Those who have not had a chance to make a s'more should make theirs as everyone else is getting settled. Announce that they all have five minutes to finish making s'mores or getting a snack or drink before the "scary story" begins.

❧ Blow your whistle to gather everyone at the fire for the "scary story."

Scary Story

❧ Once they are settled and quiet, tell the "scary story" you've chosen from one of the following resources. Be sure to choose a story that took place during the three hundred years of Roman persecution before Christianity was accepted. The story of Polycarp or the 40 Roman soldiers who froze on a lake are both examples of great "scary stories" that illustrate true Halloween heroes. Those stories and others can be found in:

- *Jesus Freaks*, Volumes I and II by dc Talk (Bethany House, 1999, 2002)
- *Foxe's Book of Martyrs* by John Foxe (Zondervan, 1978), and *The New Foxe's Book of Martyrs* (Bridge-Logos, 2001)
- *Heroic Faith* and *Extreme Devotion* by The Voice of the Martyrs (W Publishing Group, 2002)

❧ At the end of the story, talk about how that hero was able to face his situation without fear because of his or her faith in God's strength and promises. Use Matthew 10:28 as an example: "Do not fear those who kill the body but are unable to kill the soul; but rather fear Him who is able to destroy both soul and body in hell" (NASB).

❧ Talk about the biggest promise that particular hero would have counted on: the promise of eternal life.

❧ Assure the kids that they don't have to fear death, because that same promise has been given to us as well.

❧ In simple and clear terms, explain the gospel.

❧ We suggest that you give kids an opportunity to pray silently to receive Christ. If you do lead a prayer of salvation with which children could pray along silently, be sure afterward to ask them to tell you or their parents about the wonderful decision that they have made to trust in Jesus as their Savior.

❧ End the story time by celebrating the fact that "perfect love casts out fear" (1 John 4:18, NASB) and that Halloween is really a holiday of faith, not fear.

❋ Invite kids to ask questions before they leave if they are
  confused by anything you said or if they are curious to
  learn more.
❋ Remember that parents may be arriving to pick up their
  children before your story is finished, so have another
  adult waiting by the door, ready to invite them to the
  campfire and hear the story as well.

Saying Good-bye

❋ When the party ends and you have said a closing
  prayer, thank the kids for coming.
❋ There is no need to offer a party favor. (With Halloween
  on the way, they will soon be loaded down with candy.)
❋ After the party, pray with your own children that the
  message their friends heard would help them to live a
  life of faith in Christ, not fear of the unknown.

FILL-IN-THE-GAP PARTY

Kim, the Invisible Girl

T he day I dreaded all summer had finally arrived. As I sat helplessly in the car, my oldest son took his first steps into junior high. Bravely, Chase squared his ever-broadening shoulders and strode with surprising confidence away from the car, where I sat, straining to catch the last glimpse of my son as he disappeared into a sea of pubescent youth.

I'd heard stories about children who entered the portal into junior high only to be transformed from beloved children into mood swinging, hormone raging, grade slipping, grocery consuming adolescents. As one friend put it, "From the time a teenage boy enters junior high until he emerges from high school, he has effectively checked out of the human race." I could only hope that this was an exaggeration.

Even at its worst, none of that troubled me quite as much as the thought that the son I always knew and loved, once inside those halls, would vanish into thin air. In his quest for "sameness," his uniqueness would disappear. I knew the incentives were often too compelling to ignore. The goal becomes to dress alike, talk alike, and blend in at any cost. Deviation from the norm can make kids targets for those trying to sharpen their half-developed wits.

Personally, I entered seventh grade with a bull's eye on my back.

Short pants: *"Hey, Kim, expecting a flood today?"*

First perm: *"Kim stuck her finger in a light socket!"*

Didn't wash my hair: *"Hey, Kim, you saving that grease to make French fries?"*

Today I might tell such juveniles to get a life, but back then they *were* my life. I wanted to be just like everyone else, so like everyone, short pants, perms, and skipping showers were out. My theme song became "Don't rock the boat, baby." Overall, I was pretty successful at settling into an inconspicuous routine. I developed the every-teen look—straight hair, bell-bottoms, and platform shoes. I listened to The Captain and Tennille and never questioned muskrats being in love. I complained about cafeteria food I actually liked. I ignored the right people, never quoted my parents, and adopted the prevailing opinion on any and every subject.

This strategy never won me overwhelming popularity or even a large number of friends, but it took the bull's-eye off my back. I didn't want to change the world; I just wanted to be accepted by it.

Twenty-five years later, I am so thankful I remember how it felt to be there. I understand my son's struggles, what it's like to want to be the same and want to be special. Happily, Chase is doing far better than I did. In high school now, he's found a good balance. His clothes are the same as everyone else's but he holds to the faith in Christ that makes him special. He and a handful of other kids are rocking the boat, sharing their faith and inviting others to youth group and Bible studies. They don't hide their difference. They look for opportunities to invite others to join them. Of course, they carry it all out in baggy pants and shaggy hair, looking like everyone else.

It isn't always easy to stand for your beliefs. Chase will face many temptations to be like the crowd. Our goal is to strengthen him and even help him take more territory for Christ.

Strength often comes in numbers, so we are constantly grateful for the many young believers Chase has as his friends. Part of that strength comes from knowing that we stand with him, too. There is no greater privilege for a parent than "contending as one [with your child] for the faith of the gospel" (Philippians 1:27). To work hand in hand to reach out to others with the good news of Jesus Christ is not only an incredible joy, it is also a great training ground for your teenager. For us, hosting a Fill-in-the-Gap Party during the Halloween season is one way to seize that opportunity.

Fill-in-the-Gap is a party we throw at home for Chase's friends. We hold it on a night before Halloween since our two younger ones still like to go trick-or-treating. Beforehand, we sit down with Chase and plan all the details. We print invitations on the computer. The party's success depends on him because it's his responsibility to hand out invitations. He invites kids on the football team and in his drama class, acquaintances, and anyone he's gotten to know personally. A couple of his friends also help.

My husband, Tony, and I handle the details: a campfire, a hayride to a nearby cemetery, Flashlight Tag, and refreshments. We keep it simple, but with a little effort, it is an effective way to engage those hard-to-reach teens.

The main activity of the evening is visiting a nearby cemetery. Of course, we take along plenty of parents, and the kids are briefed beforehand about respectful behavior. The goal is to have them gather some information from the tombstones. Working in pairs, each team looks for the oldest gravestone, the most recent, the persons who lived the longest and the shortest, and any epitaphs that tell about that person's life. After about 15 minutes, we gather at the tombstone I've chosen to discuss.

Each pair of kids reports to the group, and after they have all shared and prizes have been handed out, I ask: "What does this tombstone tell us?" We discuss and discover that the tombstone sheds little light on the person's life. Instead, I tell them, "It's the gap between the two dates that says it all. It isn't about when you were born, or when you died, but what you do in the gap." I ask what their lives will stand for. "What is in the gap that will add real meaning and significance to the date of your death?" I tell them that what lies beyond the grave for each of us can only be decided while we are here in the gap. Using specific scriptures, I challenge the kids and invite them to make a decision to fill in the gap and examine their eternal futures.

The party is always a hit with teens. It could also be the most spiritually significant event some of them ever attend. It doesn't require a lot of effort and is appropriate for both girls and guys.

Here are some tips for hosting this fun party with your teen.

Tips for Hosting a Fill-in-the-Gap Party

Some activities are similar to the Fear-Not Party, so be sure to refer to that chapter. The party is generally appropriate for junior high through college age.

Planning
- 🍁 Talk through the aim and the activities of the party with your teenager in advance. Encourage him to be part of the planning. Brainstorm what you will need, the order of the activities, invitations, food, and distributing the invitations.
- 🍁 Let your teen come up with a plan for inviting friends. Help broaden the list by talking about her different circles: classes, sports teams, church, extracurricular activities, and neighbors.
- 🍁 Determine the date, time, and length of the party. School nights work well, and two hours allows everything without feeling rushed. We chose 6:30 to 8:30 P.M.

- 🍁 Pray with your teen for boldness and success in reaching out to others with invitations.
- 🍁 Design invitations and suggest your teen recruit a friend or friends to help distribute them. Print more than you plan on having, being certain not to leave anyone out. Many kids will not come, but the simple act of inviting them can open doors.
- 🍁 Ensure the invitation has clear directions to your home Draw a map or print one out and include a phone number. Also request they bring flashlights.

Preparing

Make advance preparations for the campfire, the hayride trip to the cemetery, and refreshments.

- 🍁 If your city code allows, making s'mores by a campfire is a great activity for a fall party. Refer to the tips given for the Fear-Not Party.
- 🍁 Set a table of snacks outside. Teens are easy to please, so store-bought cookies, popcorn, chips and dips, and drinks will be crowd-pleasers. Unlike elementary-aged children, you will want to provide more than you think you'll need. Teens are big snackers. If weather is cool, have hot chocolate and cider available. Use paper cups and plates to make cleanup easy, and set a trash container outside.
- 🍁 Have a tray ready with all the makings for s'mores: chocolate candy bars, marshmallows, graham crackers, and skewers or clothes hangers.
- 🍁 Find the nearest cemetery. Plan to caravan in exchange of the hayride if necessary. Let the groundskeeper know when you will be there. Visit beforehand to choose a headstone for presenting your devotion. Also, recruit

enough parents to help supervise. If teens are driving,
be sure they know where the cemetery is before leaving.

❧ If a cemetery is not an option, you can make several
tombstones out of cardboard or Styrofoam with humorous
names ("Kick D. Bucket," "Ima Goner," "Dee Ceased,"
etc.), dates of birth and death, and epitaphs such as
"Beloved Father," or "Precious Dentist." Set them up with
stakes outside if possible, around a yard, orchard, or field,
with the one you will use for discussion near the campfire or fireplace. Design the scavenger hunt the same as
you would for the cemetery with 20-25 tombstones.

❧ For a hayride, make arrangements for the trailer and
hay bales, and determine a safe, low-traffic route in
advance. Drive the route at the time of night you will
actually be traveling to be sure there are no surprises on
party night.

❧ Set out extra flashlights with fresh batteries for Flashlight Tag in case some people forget to bring theirs.

❧ Recruit parents for the snack table, campfire, and
games, and to accompany your group to the cemetery.

❧ Have a whistle for the game.

❧ Have plenty of different items for winners to choose
from: unique candies, toys, games, and handheld
puzzles from the dollar store.

The Games

❧ Once most people have arrived, blow your whistle and
gather everyone by the campfire. Welcome them and
introduce yourself. During the course of the night, try
to make one-on-one contact with each of them, even
just to ask their name and tell them how glad you are
they came. Explain what they will be doing and the
safety guidelines.

🍁 Start the party with Romans-versus-Christians Flash-light Tag. This will give you the opportunity to explain the real meaning of Halloween. Refer to the tips section of the Fear-Not Party for details on this game.

🍁 When the game is over, blow the whistle, and then prepare everyone for the trip to the cemetery. Remind them to take a flashlight.

🍁 Take a head count.

🍁 At the cemetery, remind kids to behave respectfully and to walk, not run.

🍁 Send them out in teams of two or three with a piece of paper and a pencil to find the earliest birth, most recent death, oldest, youngest, and something that represents the person's life.

🍁 When time is up, blow the whistle to gather around the tombstone you've chosen.

🍁 Give prizes and transition to the devotional, sharing the details of the gospel and inviting them to make a decision to trust in Christ.

🍁 Close with prayer.

🍁 Take another head count before returning home.

🍁 As the party ends, remember to let kids know how glad you are they came.

Afterward

🍁 Talk to your teen about how things went.

🍁 Pray for the seeds that were planted, asking God for opportunities to follow up with many.

🍁 Talk about ways to take advantage of any upcoming opportunities.

🍁 Thank and bless your teen for his help.

TRICKY TREATERS

Pam Resigns from Life

I had made up my mind. Life was tough; it had finally gotten the better of me. It was the year I made a claim on all of my parents' different insurance policies—except life insurance, of course. I was only 20 and it all started when another college girl, running late for work, was making up time by driving and putting on makeup simultaneously. Her eyeliner was straight but after she hit my '67 Mustang, my bumper was not. Neither of us was hurt—physically, that is. Emotionally, I was thrown for a loop when she lied to the insurance company and claimed the accident was my fault.

That very next semester my parents' health insurance was practically maxed out when my appendix ruptured, leading to emergency surgery and nine days in the hospital. The whole ordeal took me out of my spring semester at Texas Tech University for two weeks. In the midst of it, I had my doubts that I would ever go back, but with Mom's expert nursing and home cooking, I was eventually strong enough to return.

The straw that finally broke the camel's back came just months later when the kitchen burned down at my dinner party and the call was made to my parents' insurance company. Mom and Dad were out of town and I just couldn't see how I would ever recover from this final blow. It all seemed too overwhelming.

The next morning, I sat alone in their house, now permeated by the rancid smell of day-old smoke, as I waited for them to return. Rocking myself back and forth in the dark, I tried to come up with the answer to living a risk-free life. *Let's see,* I thought, *if I don't drive no one can hit me. If I don't cook there will be no fires. I can't eliminate all the health risks, but since my only appendix has been removed that's one less organ to worry about.*

My mom returned home to find me still rocking away my troubles. "Pam, what are you doing sitting in the dark?"

"I'm just going to stay right here where it's safe, Mom."

Full of compassion but also aware of my tendency to bury my head in the sand, she didn't waste any time dealing with the real issue. "Pam, you can't hide from the world. Bad things are going to happen. You can't change that; you can only keep moving forward. As long as you don't use our *life* insurance policy, you'll get through the difficult times."

If I was ever going to leave the house again, Mom's words were exactly what I needed to hear. Over the years, many things tested my courage far more than the fire or the fender bender. Through every difficulty, I have found strength and the inspiration to move forward, partly from other people, like Mom, who came alongside to encourage me. That, too, I'm sure is how many of the first Halloween heroes stood their ground. Other believers helped give them courage. Because I know what it means to lean on friends for that kind support, I have a passion for offering it to others whose faith has been rocked by life. Even more, I like to inspire children to see themselves as courage givers.

My third- through sixth-grade Sunday school girls embraced this vision with fervor. They couldn't wait to accept the challenge to be encouragers—with a slight twist. This group of girls would be *secret* encouragers. We brainstormed together about people we knew who might need a boost of courage to get through a difficult time. It didn't take long for the group to choose three names.

"Mrs. Byrd has been going through cancer treatments. My family prays for her every night. Let's encourage her," one suggested.

"This is a hard time for my grandma Linda," offered another. "It's been one year since my grandpa died. Miss Pam, I think she needs encouraging."

Then one of the girls thought of a six-year-old at our church who was struggling with fear after the World Trade Center attacks. "Reagan has been having nightmares since September 11. I bet he could use some courage."

We had our list, but our group needed a name. The girls reasoned that we would be secretly leaving our gifts of encouragement at night and that we would have to sneak and crawl through yards to avoid being seen, hence, our name would be "The Night Crawlers."

First we created a card for each one of the people we selected. They included words of encouragement for what that person was going through and Bible verses to strengthen them. We also prayed for each and packed a goodie bag to leave at their doorstep with the card signed The Night Crawlers.

The excitement was electric. As we pulled into the first neighborhood, we had to park several houses away to avoid detection. This was the best part. There is nothing like crawling through the bushes, hiding from cars, and feeding dogs treats to keep them quiet. The hardest thing was preventing the giggling from giving us away. Once all 10 Night Crawlers made it to the doorstep and the basket was in place, we rang the doorbell and made a break for it.

When all three missions were accomplished, we agreed the night had been a huge success. It took several weeks for the excitement to wear off from encouraging others. They talked about it every time we were together. They weren't the only ones talking either. Somehow word got out that The Night Crawlers were part of our Sunday school class and soon we received letters from our encouragement targets. The girls were even more excited once they found out how their efforts had affected others. Linda wrote to the girls:

> *To The Night Crawlers,*
> *What a wonderful surprise your words of encouragement were and how wonderfully timed. This September has not been my finest hour! I had another birthday and was feeling older, my husband's death was one year ago this month, and then there was our nation's disaster in New York. Just at a low point—the Night Crawlers struck—leaving me little bits of love scattered all around. It reminded me that life was not over—it is merely another season. I'll now look a little harder for those everyday treasures.*
>
> *Thank you, Night Crawlers.*

Each of the people we chose to encourage was dealing with difficult circumstances that could have resulted in fear or a faltering faith. Our actions were just one little way to communicate the message of hope and give them strength. In return, each, in their own words, expressed what Paul experienced: "Your love has given me great joy and encouragement, because you, brother, have refreshed the hearts of the saints" (Philemon 7).

What a blessing that our simple acts could "refresh the heart." The only regret we had about our escapade of encouragement was the name we chose for our group. It didn't cross our minds at the time that a little boy dealing with fear shouldn't get a note signed by "The Night Crawlers." The next year we changed our name to "The Encouragement Crew."

If those who already understand the ever-present help of God are helped by acts of encouragement, imagine how it might strengthen your unsaved friend, neighbor, or coworker who is experiencing a trial. We may never be called to go to a burning stake or face prison to demonstrate that our faith is real, but would you be willing to crawl through the bushes? This Halloween, instead of just trick-or-treating with your family, be *a tricky treater*. Who knows? It may become a family Halloween tradition. Best of all, it might be just the thing to bring "much joy and comfort . . . to refresh the heart" in a season that celebrates the power of faith.

TIPS FOR TRICKY TREATERS

Planning

- Talk as a family about the benefits of encouraging others. Look together at verses like 1 Thessalonians 5:11, Hebrews 3:13, Philemon 7.
- Think of people you might encourage: Other believers, friends, or pastors are a great start. Tricky treating is also a great way to communicate the love of God to unbelievers. Add the name of at least one person who doesn't already know Christ as Savior.
- Pray for the people on your list. Ask God to show you how best to encourage him or her.
- Remind your children that we have salvation because Jesus offered it as a free gift, just as you are offering a free gift of encouragement to others.

Preparing

- Be mindful of the person's specific circumstance. Remember, they don't need an expensive gift, just generous encouragement. Little things will be just as meaningful.

❦ Some treats are: special foods, something to pamper themselves, a devotional book, and any creative items that show you thought specifically about them.

❦ A fun way to encourage is with a candy bar message. Using candy bars glued to poster board, send a message like this one: "I'm so happy when I think of you, I'm overcome with *Snickers*. You shine brighter than the *Milky Way*. You are worth more to me than a *100 Grand*. You make my day better than any *Payday*. With lots of *Hugs* and *Kisses*."

❦ Include a card that mentions things you appreciate about them, words of encouragement, or scriptures for comfort, courage, or peace.

❦ Write your names on the card going to the person who does not know Christ. It will open doors for deeper relationships.

❦ Decide if you will give your gift anonymously to the Christian. You may want to discuss with your family Matthew 6:2, which urges us not to brag about our good works to get credit from men. God, who sees, also rewards.

Delivering

❦ Have fun going on an adventure to trick the person by leaving the treat secretly. This added aspect of sneaking to deliver the package will show your children how much fun it can be to encourage others.

❦ If you have time, make a celebration out of it. Stop for ice cream or a hot drink on the way home.

❦ When you get home, pray that the person will be blessed and will thank *God* as a response to the encouragement.

TEAM TEACHING

Getting in Shape with Kim

Never in a million years would my ninth-grade gym teacher believe that for one year I became a girls' PE coach. It was truly an amazing transformation.

There is no bigger oxymoron than "Coach Kim." I don't enjoy sweating. I know next to nothing about sports, I can't tell the difference between running shoes and sneakers, and to me, "cross trainers" are people who go to seminary. So what possessed me to accept a position to coach girls' PE at my children's school for an entire year?

That's what I was asking soon after agreeing. I planned to meet the boys' gym teacher, Coach Sherrie, a few days before school started to help clean out the equipment room. Preparing for some good manual labor, I dressed in my old shorts, ball cap, and a shirt that was stained and pre-wrinkled. Perfect for a work day. Not so perfect for a school-wide teacher work day in which all the teachers would be present wearing matching, embroidered pant suits, perfectly starched blouses, and—my favorite— a little capri number with beaded fringe. Remember what I was wearing?

I was seriously questioning what I was doing there (and I'm sure I wasn't the only one). It wasn't just my poor fashion taste and inexperience that brought my qualifications into doubt.

There was also the business of my less-than-impressive PE past.

The only student in ninth grade to flunk physical education, I always brought up the rear in laps. I was the last girl picked for teams, and not even a double Twinkie bribe could get me a partner in bowling. I even warmed the bench in square dancing. Truthfully, I preferred it that way. I liked the bench—so much, in fact, I often wouldn't dress out for gym, hoping I'd just be sent to my favorite spot on the bleachers where I could avoid sweating, and thereby avoid that whole communal shower experience.

In light of all that, it's inconceivable why I would volunteer to endure 95-degree weather to lead anyone in the pursuit of physical fitness. I'd spent my entire life circumventing that very thing. For Pete's sake, I don't even go to the end of the driveway to get the mail without the aid of my son's scooter.

How can I explain my change of heart? There is but one answer. I loved those kids. If this was a way to contribute to their lives, so be it. I was willing. Realistically, though, I knew that love alone would not make me capable. I owe that to Coach Sherrie. Her experience and knowledge enabled me to do things I otherwise could not have. She provided the resources and help that transformed a PE dropout into a PE professional—in the loosest sense of the word, of course. Together we challenged, trained, and helped those kids grow in character as well as fitness. Working as a team, everyone benefited.

Hopefully, the teachers at your child's school are infinitely more prepared than I was, but the lesson about teamwork is one we can all apply. "Two are better than one, because they have a good return for their work" (Ecclesiastes 4:9).

There are so many ways we can support the educators who invest in our children. Send an occasional note of thanks. Volunteer as a classroom aid or field-trip chaperone. Help with a class party or special event. Teachers have the same goals we do when it comes to our children: They want them to grow intellectually and in maturity. When we offer practical help, we work together in that goal.

Halloween offers a unique opportunity for parents to come alongside teachers with help and resources to capitalize on the redeeming aspects of the holiday. With respect for the teacher, the school, and state regulations, the origins of Halloween can be presented in a way that teaches historical truths without crossing the line into "religious training."

Many teachers have not had the opportunity to study the origins of Halloween, and they don't have an accurate understanding of what to do with a holiday that seems based mostly on superstition. Offering historical facts about the holiday could be greatly appreciated. Simply by sharing the facts about Halloween (see "Halloween's True Story") and encouraging a few appropriate activities, you can help to teach about the historical origin of Halloween.

Make the offer graciously, with a true servant's spirit, keeping in mind that while you may be excited about what you have to offer, it is left entirely to the teacher's discretion about how to receive it. Your role is simply to offer. A great way to approach this is to meet privately at a convenient time and say something like, "Miss _____, I have come across some of the little-known facts about the historical origin of Halloween. I would love to provide a classroom party or activity time during the month of October. Could I share what I have in mind with you?"

By asking rather than just showing up with your resources ready to take over, you can give the teacher the opportunity to decide whether or not to use your help. Take the initiative but leave the results to God. If the teacher is not interested, be gracious and let her know that you appreciate what she does for your children and you'd be willing to help some other time. Honoring your teacher's wishes either way will communicate respect and may be the very thing that opens doors in the future. If the teacher agrees, use one or more of the following ideas.

TIPS FOR TEACHING ABOUT HALLOWEEN IN THE CLASSROOM

Classroom Activities

🍁 Students can work individually or in groups on this activity using the "traditional" elements of Halloween to learn how we must work to recover truth from superstition. It could also make for a good oral presentation on the day of a Halloween party.

- Each student (or group) is given one Halloween "creature" to discover some facts about: bats, spiders, skeletons, black cats, pumpkins, witches, ghosts, goblins, werewolves, vampires, or mummies.

- On the day of the party, the student or groups will share the good qualities of their creature ("bats are very useful," "pumpkins are a fruit") and how they differ from the common perception.

- Each student should be asked to summarize what he or she learned about the differences between superstition and truth.

- Have children get creative: Each student or group could be responsible for bringing a decoration to the party using their Halloween creature, or create a game where the teacher could read aloud a few facts written by each student group about their Halloween creature to try to stump the class. (For example: "There are nine hundred kinds of me in the world. What am I?" Answer: Bats.) Simple prizes or candies could be given for correct answers.

🍁 Tell the history behind the first Halloween from the chapter "Halloween's True Story."

- Ask the children if they have ever seen or heard of someone being treated badly for what he or she believed. The treatment of the Jews during World War II is a more recent example.
- Give the facts about Roman persecution and a documented story of a particular hero from that three hundred years of persecution.
- Allow kids to talk about their feelings about that kind of treatment of others. Ask, "Why do you think people sometimes treat others badly?" "What might happen if people understood the truth about others instead of holding to superstitions?"
- Talk about why it's important to study history and to remember the difference between truth and superstition.

❁ Use the tale of Jack O'Lantern from pages 38-39 to teach about fables.
- Explain that fables are stories not always founded in reality that teach a moral.
- Tell the tale of Jack O'Lantern. Ask the children to see if they can find the moral.
- Have students fill brown lunch bags with shredded paper and draw the face of Stingy Old Jack on them.
- Encourage the kids to write a fable of their own that teaches a moral.

❁ Teach the origins of Halloween costumes and trick-or-treating. (See the chapter "Trick or Treat.")
- Since Halloween originated as a holiday to remember "heroes," allow kids to dress up as a hero they admire and tell what quality makes that hero special.
- In the spirit of the original mumming tradition that included performing for treats door-to-door, allow kids to think up short plays for the characters they

represent. Ask each child if he or she imitates that
character in real life and how.

❊ Study some of the themes behind Halloween.

- Discuss the word *persecution.* Ask the kids what kind
  of people today are persecuted or mistreated for their
  beliefs. Study a country where people are currently
  living under persecution. Explain that many religious
  groups—including the one at the heart of the first
  Halloween, Christianity—are still being persecuted.

- Considering how Rome treated Christians prior to
  A.D. 300, why are civil and constitutional rights so
  important? How are we all protected today from the
  treatment Christians went through almost two thousand years ago? Share what our constitutional rights
  are in regard to religion from the Bill of Rights,
  Amendment I: "Congress shall make no law respect-
  ing an establishment of religion, or prohibiting the
  free exercise thereof . . ." (see www.memory.loc.gov/
  const/bor.html for more).

- Since Halloween and All Saints' Day were meant as
  days to think about the examples set by others, discuss someone who has set a good example, either
  known to the students or a public figure. Let students
  share who they most want to emulate.

- Some other themes to teach on are "tolerance for
  others' faith," "respect for the rights of others,"
  "respect for authority vs. respect for God," "what to
  do in scary situations," and "sticking to your beliefs."

❊ Telephone Game: Teach about the importance of accuracy and truth, showing how anything, even holidays,
can easily become distorted when passed from person
to person over time.

- Whisper to the first student, "This Halloween, I think I'll stick to the truth."
- Have the student whisper what he thinks you said to the next.
- The last person tells the group what phrase he thinks he heard.
- Explain that over time, the truth can become distorted.
- Use this to teach how history, like that of Halloween, has been mixed up over time (refer to "Halloween's True Story").

Decorations and Party Ideas

- Use "traditional" items, such as bats, but hang "speech bubbles" with the items telling a true fact. For instance, a bat's speech bubble could read: "I can eat 600 mosquitoes an hour." A skeleton could say, "I can't talk. I have no voice box."
- Decorate the room with "heroes" in the spirit of the original Halloween.
- Have a poster of the Bill of Rights, and especially the First Amendment.
- Have healthy snacks available, like dried cranberry mix, popcorn balls, and toasted pumpkin seeds.
- With party favors, be creative and give something that focuses on qualities worth emulating, or even little Bill of Rights scrolls or something patriotic.

What Is Permitted in Public Schools

- Start by reassuring the teacher of the legality of teaching about the religious history of holidays when the purpose is providing instruction about historical tradition rather than promoting particular religious beliefs. That is according to Federal Court ruling Florey vs. Sioux Falls School District, 8th Circuit, 1980.

🍁 If there are further questions, visit the American Center for Law and Justice at www.aclj.org. In the search box, type in "religious holidays" for information to pass on to teachers or school districts.

Commemorating the Faithful

*The things which you have heard from me
in the presence of many witnesses,
entrust these to faithful men
who will be able to teach others also.*
—2 TIMOTHY 2:2, NASB

HARVEST BOXES

Kim's Español es Stinky

A stranger arrived at our house one evening about nine o'clock. With an inviting smile and a heavy Spanish accent he extended his hand and said, "I am Caleb."

This was the moment our kids had been waiting for since we volunteered to host this guest for our church's missions conference. Finally, there he stood, as we greeted him eagerly and bombarded him with questions.

"Where are you from?" "Do you have any kids?" "Do you like dogs?"

Caleb, still perfecting his English, understood us as long as we talked slowly. My husband, however, also added volume, a Spanish accent, and a few Spanish words. Raised in El Paso, Tony felt it was a good opportunity to brush up on his "second language."

Loudly, he said things like, "Our niños just got to our casa from playing bas-a-ball." (Somehow an Italian accent slipped in.)

I employed the more subtle sign language. Like a bizarre game of charades, Caleb worked to decipher my too quick English and flailing hand motions. He, more relaxed, communicated competently, even with his endearing misuse of verb tenses.

All of our attention seemed to entertain Caleb immensely.

Soon, he was correcting Tony's Spanish and telling the kids all about his life growing up in South America.

Caleb had been a lawyer in Bolivia before committing his life to Christ five years earlier. It was then that he felt called to preach the gospel. He shared Christ with the Indian workers in the coca fields of Bolivia until God led him to seminary in South Texas, where he had just graduated.

For all his education, though, we discovered there was one thing Caleb knew nothing about: baseball. The next day, with a Wiffle ball and paper plates for bases, the kids taught Caleb America's favorite pastime. For an hour, our backyard was converted into spring training camp. It was kids versus adults, with Caleb as the rookie. He pitched, hit a home run, and even umpired, calling with his thick accent, "Striking three! You are out of there!"

Though he had a great time, we were certain baseball was not his calling. His was to the harvest where the fields were ripe. God had opened the door for Caleb to begin a mission in the Rio Grande Valley, serving on monthly financial support totalling less than one of our monthly car payments. Yet, with few possessions and even fewer resources, he seemed certain God would provide all that was needed.

After all, God specializes in providing in unexpected ways. For example, out of the blue, it occurred to Tony he had several business suits that no longer fit, and if altered might work for Caleb as he began his ministry. As he searched his closet, he also found belts, jeans, and new shoes he couldn't wear.

One by one, Caleb tried on each item, finding that they all fit as if they had been tailor-made for him. We all realized that God had planned it all along. Who else could have orchestrated a lawyer from Bolivia wearing my husband's suits as he preached the gospel to Mexican immigrants in South Texas? Only God.

With tears of thanksgiving, Caleb praised God for His provision and thanked us as well. We were thankful, too, that in His mercy, God did not let us miss "the privilege of sharing in this service to the saints" (2 Corinthians 8:4). Though a small thing in our estimation, God has made it a holy calling.

> Dear friend, you are faithful in what you are doing for
> the brothers, even though they are strangers to you . . .
> You will do well to send them on their way in a manner
> worthy of God. It was for the sake of the Name that
> they went out, receiving no help from the pagans. We
> ought therefore to show hospitality to such men so that
> we may work together for the truth. (3 John 5-9, emphasis
> added)

Even more, Paul clarifies that there is great blessing for those giving as well as those going.

> You sent me aid again and again when I was in need. Not
> that I am looking for a gift, but I am looking for what may
> be credited to your *account*. . . . [Your gifts] are a fragrant
> offering, an acceptable sacrifice, pleasing to God. (Philippi-
> ans 4:16-18, emphasis added)

God's hand is extended to both the sender and the worker, inviting each one to join in His harvest. The Halloween season is a perfect time for families to accept that invitation and send a Harvest Box to one of God's "field workers."

Making Harvest Boxes isn't an idea that focuses on the bounty of the land, but on the bounty of God in relentlessly pursuing those who would be harvested into His kingdom around the world. For that, He has called many workers to leave their homes and families, who often suffer as His ambassadors of the Good News. Our part can be to extend to them encouragement and practical help, the very thing Paul urges us to do.

> "Welcome [such a person] in the Lord with great joy, and honor men like him, because he almost died for the work of Christ, risking his life. . . ." (Philippians 2:29-30)

Here is something we can do: simply send a box of items to a missionary. They can be practical items that may be hard to come by, or treats to encourage them. It is a family project and something you can do with your church. Accept God's invitation to join in the work, and remember Paul's words: "I am looking for what may be credited to your account." This Halloween season, send a Harvest Box and commemorate the ongoing work of the faithful.

TIPS FOR HARVEST BOXES

Planning

- 🍁 Ask your missionary for a wish list of items. You may be surprised at the simple things that they would consider a luxury. For instance, Girl Scout cookies, their favorite deodorant, and even a metropolitan newspaper could be real treats.
- 🍁 Harvest Boxes have an added blessing since they typically arrive in time for the Christmas holidays. Find out at your post office how long it will take for your package to arrive, and consider making it a Christmassy encouragement.
- 🍁 Don't worry that by asking them you will be obligated to provide everything on the list. They will be pleased with whatever you send.

In addition to asking about a wish list, inquire about what may be illegal. For instance, in a country closed to the gospel, you should not send religious materials that would endanger them.

Ask about customs regulations and postage costs.

Ask about restrictions on the declared value of the box you send. In some countries, if a box has a declared value over $40, it is taxed too high to be acceptable Your missionary will know what the exact requirements are and can make suggestions about packaging.

Also ask before sending any food items. It takes a long time for packages to get to some countries and foods may be stale, eaten by bugs, or spoiled by the time they arrive.

Preparing

Encourage your children to contribute financially from their allowance so that they can reap the spiritual blessings.

Younger children can also contribute by making home-made cards or gifts.

Set aside time for your entire family to write personal notes of encouragement to the missionaries, being careful to observe any content restrictions. This is the biggest encouragement to those in the field. Mention ways you have been praying for them and their work. If you cannot say you have been praying, tell them you have been "thinking" of them, in quotes. They will know what you mean.

Talk to your children about why you would have to be careful about what you send to some countries.

Make it a family event by going as a family to shop for the items on the wish list.

Creative Ideas

- 🍁 Include some current event items: news magazines, metro newspapers, entertainment magazines, their own local newspapers or clippings.
- 🍁 Many missionaries are hungry for solid Bible teaching and encouragement for themselves. If allowed, send teaching tapes from their favorite pastor, books, devotionals, or even Bible study materials.
- 🍁 Send Christian music cassettes or CDs.
- 🍁 Many missionaries miss being able to make their favorite dishes. Many of our friends ask specifically for items to make Mexican food. Check with your missionary or sponsor organization to see if food items are permitted.
- 🍁 If they have children, kids' videos, books, and even comic strips are always welcome. If you are sending videocassettes, find out about VCR compatibility.
- 🍁 Candies are always a big hit with children.
- 🍁 If there is a new cultural trend here in the U.S., send along such an item so that the kids get a flavor of home.
- 🍁 Send a picture of your family.
- 🍁 Tag at least one item with the specific name of each person in the missionary family. It will make them feel special and remembered.

Sending

- 🍁 Package your items in a durable box, especially for overseas mailing.
- 🍁 Be sure to address it exactly as the missionary has indicated to ensure it arrives.
- 🍁 As a family, set aside time to pray together over the box as you prepare to send it. Be sure to thank God for the

opportunity to contribute to His work by encouraging and meeting the needs of His workers.

🍁 Don't expect an immediate response. It can take a while for packages to travel, but do let the missionary know to expect the package.

🍁 The biggest thing is to just do it. Out of sight shouldn't mean out of mind where our co-laborers in Christ are concerned!

HEROES

Kim, Pam, and the Duke

My heroes have always been cowboys."

The old country-and-western song was certainly true for us. Raised in different parts of Texas, Pam and I share common ground in our hero, the most famous cowboy of them all, John Wayne. We discovered our similar admiration for the Duke when we were invited to speak at a conference center that replicated the Alamo. As we took the stage, we noticed that standing just to our right and also facing the audience was a life-sized stand-up of the big guy himself. It was a race to see which of us would have her picture taken with him first. The highlight of our trip was definitely speaking at "The Alamo" with John Wayne at our sides!

On the way home we swapped accounts of our hero.

"What was your favorite movie?"

"Can you do his swagger?"

"Were you a member of his fan club?"

"Did you ever write him a letter?"

We both had written, but only one of us was fortunate enough to get an autographed picture in return. Of course, who needed a picture? So many of his movie moments were etched into our minds.

Growing up in the 70s, there weren't many larger-than-life heroes to choose. Donny Osmond had moves, Clint Eastwood had the brawn, but the Duke had magic to transport us into a world of unquestioning courage.

In *The Cowboys* he quipped to the young riders to get going: "We're burnin' daylight!" Or in *The Quiet Man:* "Mister, if you count to three, you'll never hear the man say ten." You knew he meant every word he said because, well, he was John Wayne. That wasn't easy to forget no matter what character he was playing. There was just something about this man that told you he was rock solid.

Wayne was a powerful and unforgettable persona. Jimmy Stewart said, "I can't imagine there's anyone in the country who doesn't know who he is. Kids will be talking about him long after the rest of us are gone. John will make the history books . . . because he worked and lived his life to reflect the ideals of his country" (James Stewart, *John Wayne: A Tribute* [Austin, Texas: Holt, Rinehart and Winston, 1982]).

We couldn't express our feelings that eloquently as kids, but all those admirable qualities were like a magnet, drawing us to something we would rarely encounter in the real world—selfless heroism. Best of all, he was all our own—not a James Bond from England or a superhero from Krypton. He was all-American. In fact, it's been said that no one will ever be as American as John Wayne and the whole world knew it. When he died on June 11, 1979, a Tokyo newspaper headline read, "Mr. America Passes On."

There was never a hero quite like him and there will never be another. John Wayne was one of a kind—and that is at once a great fact and a pity. John Wayne, the hero, existed only in the imaginary world of movies. What we saw and loved about him was an act. We couldn't really expect to be like our childhood hero because he didn't really exist—at least not as we knew him. As fun as it was to "play" John Wayne, it is real-life heroes from whom we can draw courage or inspiration for daily living. People who live lives of character and consistency in the real world inspire us to be more and overcome more than we might have dreamed on our own. Their qualities we can realistically strive to emulate, because they've been tested in real life circumstances.

Such a hero changed Pam forever:

The whole world knew him as the founder of Campus Crusade, but I knew him as one of the most significant mentors of my life.

We marveled at God's timing that we would all be together at a staff conference when the news came of Dr. Bill Bright's home-going. As a staff "family," five thousand of us celebrated his coronation into Jesus' presence of which he had often spoken. It was a time of many mixed emotions: grieving our loss, rejoicing for his gain, and for me, reflecting on all I had learned from this amazing, humble man. So many lessons: He shared wisdom on living the Spirit-filled life, yielding to God's call, and the philosophy of win, build, and send, just to name a few.

But what truly changed my life was his perspective of God-ordained encounters. Dr. Bright always said that anytime he was able to spend at least five minutes with someone, it was his divine opportunity to tell him or her about the Savior. He didn't have a canned formula, just a sincere desire. He never wanted to walk away having missed a chance. Watching him live that philosophy challenged me. Because of his example, I try to leave a taste of the Savior with everyone I meet.

I memorized his words, made them my own, and
taught them to others. We never spent time together,
but for over 20 years I drank in his words, watching the
consistency of his life, his steadfastness, and the fruit of
his faith.

Heroes are more than characters in movies or comic books.
Like Dr. Bright, they are men and women whose lives of faith
spur us on. While such heroes are found today, many past lives
can still inspire and challenge us in our Christian journey. Halloween's historical roots make this season a wonderful time to be
introduced to some of these heroes. Their stories may be the
inspiration your children find challenging their own faith on to
greater heights one day.

During the four weeks of October, discover a few heroes
from a different time in history. One week, explore the life of a
biblical saint. The next, study someone from early church history. The third, read about a hero from the Reformation. The
final week, find out about someone still living the Christian
adventure in the world.

Remember your leaders, who spoke the word of God to you.
Consider the outcome of their way of life and imitate their
faith. (Hebrews 13:7)

This is the call at the very heart of Halloween—the time created to help us remember. Halloween is the Memorial Day of the
Christian faith. It is a time to remember those who gave their
lives for their Savior. Christ alone is worthy of our worship, but
there is much to learn from the example of those who loved and
served Him. Carefully consider "their way of life and imitate
their faith" as a family.

TIPS FOR COMMEMORATING FAITH HEROES

Heroes to Consider

- First week of October: a biblical hero who risked or lost his or her life for the faith: Esther; Daniel; Shadrach, Meshach, and Abednego; Stephen; Paul.
- Second week of October: an early church hero whose life was pivotal in the establishment of the Christian faith in the world: Polycarp, Justin Martyr, Ignatius, Tertullian
- Third week of October: A hero from the Reformation Age who helped initiate worldwide revival and the rediscovery of the gospel truths: Martin Luther, Jon Hus, William Tyndale, John Wesley, John Calvin.
- Fourth week of October: A twentieth-century or currently living hero committed to the gospel at any cost: Eric Liddell, Jim Elliot, Dietrich Bonhoeffer, Kim Jones, Dayna Curry and Heather Mercer, and current missionaries serving at risk around the world.

Resources

- A helpful place to start is the list of names found in Hebrews 11; use the cross-references to corresponding passages.
- *The New Foxe's Book of Martyrs,* by John Foxe, rewritten by Harold J. Chadwick (Bridge-Logos, 2001)
- *Jesus Freaks,* Volumes I and II, by dc Talk and The Voice of the Martyrs
- *Voice of the Martyrs* magazine or Web site (www.persecution.com)
- www.WilliamTyndale.com (William Tyndale is also covered in *Foxe's Book of Martyrs.*)
- *70 Great Christians,* by Geoffrey Hanks (Evangelical Press, 1993)

❧ Search the library, resource catalogs, or Internet on specific names mentioned above.

Learning to Imitate

❧ Focus on one faith hero at a time.

❧ Learn from their biography.

❧ Focus on their sacrificial life.

❧ Identify qualities they portrayed (courage, boldness, patience, love).

❧ Discuss how Christ displayed that quality and look at scriptures whenever possible.

❧ Discuss personal struggles encountered in living our faith.

❧ Talk about how a particular quality could be displayed in a particular circumstance.

❧ Brainstorm the most important lessons you learned from the life of that hero.

❧ Pray together that your faith would increase from that hero's example.

❧ Over the week, catch your children doing good and encourage them in imitating that kind of faith.

How, When, and Where

❧ Don't become overwhelmed trying to learn about every hero. Select one from each of the four categories listed and start there. If four is too many, choose one or two heroes. If there has been a book written by or about them that would be age appropriate, make it your bedtime reading each night for the month.

❧ Reserve a devotional time at dinner or on Sunday evenings.

❧ Point out a particular quality or detail from a hero's life and pray that during the day (or coming days) your child will have the opportunity to imitate that trait.

🍁 If you have older children or you home school, allow kids to choose someone to learn about and present to the family at a later date.

🍁 Other ideas: Make a scrapbook with pictures from magazines that represent aspects of the life of your hero; watch a film about the person; learn details about the country in which they lived; pray nightly that your children would exhibit the attributes they see in that person.

ALL SAINTS' DAY

Pam's Yo-Yo Tablecloth Treasure

If your house burned down tomorrow and you could only save a few things, what would they be?

After 17 years of marriage, my husband and I have accumulated a few nice things. Our china, our antiques, and I am quite fond of the few pieces of jewelry I own. It's a shame none of those things made the "must save" list.

What would be snatched up if flames were licking at my heels? My scrapbooks of Connor and Madison, the portraits, the memento quilt my family made when I got married, and certainly, Grandmother Rene's yo-yo pattern tablecloth.

Much of my married life has been spent protecting it from harm. Yet determined not to store it away, her beautiful handiwork covers our kitchen table with all the charm of Mother Rene herself. It's a risk, especially with my son's penchant for spilling. To date, grape juice and Kool-Aid have been added to its original pink-and-white pattern. Still, I won't put it away. Numerous times a day, I'll walk past it and be reminded of the woman who spent hours lovingly stitching each piece into a one-of-a-kind gift, as unique and original as she was.

Our home in Lubbock, Texas, was two and a half hours from Mother Rene's house in Haskell. For a city girl, there was nothing exciting about Haskell—at all. There was no movie theater, the television only picked up two channels, and there was no one to play with except my own siblings. None of that mattered though, because Mother Rene was there—and so, frequently, were we as well.

At Mother Rene's, certain things were a given, like the candy dish always being full. If it wasn't my favorite candies, it would be filled with fresh-shelled pecans from her yard. There would also be plenty of bottled Coke to go around (probably because the well water wasn't fit to drink).

My grandmother was the hardest worker I ever knew. She never stood still, cooking, sewing, picking vegetables from the garden, or any other thing she thought might make our visit more special. I always felt she was working for us, and I could see she loved it. I have seen her sew little circular yo-yo pieces together for a quilt or a tablecloth until her fingers were so stiff she couldn't straighten them anymore. She'd simply ask for help preparing a paraffin soak for her hands and then promptly get back to work.

Mother Rene was our family's treasure.

When she died, we were heartbroken. She'd been ill for years, but still we weren't prepared. I wondered over and over if she'd known how I felt about her. I ached to tell her I wanted to be just like her when I grew up: selfless. I wanted to give without expecting appreciation and to sacrifice for those I love.

She'd taught me what that looked like.

Just for me, she had hand stitched that yo-yo tablecloth, putting it together piece by piece. The pattern is flawless. It is of inestimable valuable because it holds a reminder of its maker.

That same reason should be why we honor the lives of Christians. Their lives are our reminder of the One who knit us together, stitch by stitch, into a pattern chosen to represent Him. Saints are treasures, not in who they are, but in the One they represent. It is the Maker alone who is worthy of our worship. He is our real treasure. His saints merely remind us He is the One worth living and dying for, and we honor them best when we focus on Christ.

After you have spent the month looking at heroes worthy to emulate, we suggest spending All Saints' Day experiencing the worthiness of God Himself. Paul, also a martyr of the faith, directed all men to do that very thing: "Follow my example, as I follow the example of Christ" (1 Corinthians 11:1).

What the faithful before us preached was one unchanging God who has revealed Himself to us through His Son, Jesus Christ, that we might know Him personally. Honoring that truth is a great way to also honor those who died for it.

October 31 is an exciting night, but All Saints' Day should be a day of honor. Like Christmas Eve to Christmas Day, they go hand in hand. Commemorate the day with some of the creative ideas we've compiled. Each is a simple way for your family to appreciate the one true Treasure in every season.

TIPS FOR CELEBRATING ALL SAINTS' DAY
🍁 **"God Is Great" Game** (ages 5-12)

"Through him all things were made; without him nothing was made that has been made." John 1:3

This game emphasizes that only God's creative power could have made the universe and only He is worthy to be worshiped.

- The game begins by saying, "God is great. He made . . ." Played in a round, the first person says one thing that God has made beginning with the letter A—for example, "apples."

- The second person then says, "God is great. He made apples and . . ." He or she would add something God made that begins with the letter *B*—for example, "butterflies."
- The game continues, with each person reciting the list and adding something God made with the next letter of the alphabet, until you reach the letter *Z*.

❧ Popcorn Praise (all ages)

"My mouth is filled with your praise, declaring your splendor all day long." Psalm 71:8

- "Popcorn praise" is short descriptions of God that just pop out.
- Again, use the alphabet to help kids come up with a variety of words to describe God. For example: "God, You are 'amazing.' God, You are 'beautiful.' God, You are 'crowned with glory.' God, You are better than 'diamonds.' "
- Each person can say a praise as it comes, or you can go around in a circle.
- The goal is not to finish the alphabet, but to see the vastness of God and adopt an attitude of praise.

❧ Worship Through Song (all ages)

"Praise the LORD. How good it is to sing praises to our God, how pleasant and fitting to praise him!" Psalm 147:1

- Locate the words to hymns or choruses that focus on the worthiness of God.
- As a family read and talk about the words together so that your family can understand the meaning and truths.
- Sing a few of the songs as an offering of worship.

❧ Worship Through the Psalms (all ages)

"Great is the LORD and most worthy of praise; his greatness no one can fathom." Psalm 145:3

- Talk about how many ways there are to praise God (e.g., songs, prayer, poetry) and that psalms were poems or songs written to and about God.
- Read one or two psalms that focus on the greatness of God. (Psalms 105 and 147 are good examples.)
- Give each person a piece of paper and a pen or pencil with instructions to write a poem to God. Very young children can draw a picture of praise.
- After a few minutes, read them to one another.

❧ The Art of Praise and Worship (ages 3-12)

"But be glad and rejoice forever in what I create." Isaiah 65:18

- Obtain a book of religious artwork from the library or your local Christian bookstore.
- Sit together and talk about the pictures and what stories (if any) from the Bible they represent.
- Use some creative art supplies (pens, paint, clay, etc.) for everyone to use to create something honoring God (a depiction of a Bible story, a picture of Jesus, something from creation He made, or a depiction of an emotion or feeling He evokes).
- Have an art show, allowing each to describe their artwork.
- Talk about God's pleasure in seeing our abilities, gifts, and talents used for Him. Explain that our art does not need to be in a book or gain applause from others for God to notice and remember.
- Display your family's finished art in your home.

✹ Making Praise and Worship Your "Nature"

"For since the creation of the world God's invisible quali-ties—his eternal power and divine nature—have been clearly seen, being understood from what has been made, so that men are without excuse." Romans 1:20

- Go on a nature hike and talk about the amazing diversity of God's creation. Look for bugs, unusual plants, birds, and other things that show the variety in nature. Be sure to include how "fearfully and won-derfully" He has created us (Psalm 139:14).
- After dinner, spread a blanket on your front lawn to stargaze. Talk about the vastness of the universe and how God says He has named each star.
- Turn cloud watching into a praise that Christ will one day come in the clouds to take us to heaven. Talk about the first time Jesus came and how things will be different when He returns.

LUTHER'S LEGACY

Pam and Speed Racer

D riving on the autobahn in Germany is probably every man's dream. With an overseas trip on the horizon, it was certainly my husband's. Jerry saw the promise of "no speed restrictions" as his chance at NASCAR. I saw it as an accident waiting to happen. He must have sensed my reservations, because when the time finally came for us to spend two days in Germany, he made an offer I couldn't refuse. We were traveling with our good friend Cheryl, and he counted on her support of his plan.

"I'll make you two a deal. I'll take you shopping in as many little towns and villages as you'd like to go. I'll even carry your bags for you. All I want is two things: to drive on the autobahn at whatever speed I want, and to stop in the city of Wittenberg to see the door of the Castle Church [where his hero Martin Luther nailed his 95 theses and began the Reformation]. Have we got a deal?" he asked.

Risk our lives for all-day shopping and a personal valet? "You're on!" Cheryl and I agreed.

Jerry took the phrase "no speed limit" quite seriously. My time on the autobahn was spent pleading with God to let me see my children again. I was practically green with fright—and queasiness. It was only the prospect of shopping in quaint German villages that kept me from tossing my lunch. Cheryl, on the other hand, wanted her turn behind the wheel.

Yet I hung on, convincing myself the shopping would be worth it. I was glad I did. We had the best time finding bargains and choosing distinctly German souvenirs. The best part was Jerry right there to chauffeur us from village to village.

We ended our little adventure in Wittenberg, where Jerry got down to business looking for Castle Church. We wandered through the area of town where we were told the church was located. Tracing and retracing our steps, we could not find it. In very broken German, we asked everyone we saw, finally finding someone who pointed behind us. Immediately, we saw why we hadn't been able to locate it. So surrounded by scaffolding, the church was completely obscured. A massive restoration effort was underway.

The church was inaccessible and the door Jerry had so wanted to find had been replaced. His dream was turning to crumbled bits before our eyes. Poor Jerry was beyond disappointment. Yet determined to find a way in, and undeterred by the numerous "Do Not Enter" signs, Jerry found a side door. Stepping inside was like stepping back in time.

A choir rehearsed a breathtaking chorus in the beautiful vaulted sanctuary. We could almost imagine being back in the 1500s. Seeing Jerry's face, I knew he was satisfied. I could see in his eyes he was thinking about Luther and all he had read of the great Reformer. He picked up the pen to sign the guest book as I looked on. In honor of his greatest faith hero, he wrote, "Grace Alone. Faith Alone. Christ Alone. Jerry McCune, Nacogdoches, Texas." As we turned to leave, I noticed Jerry had tears in his eyes. It wasn't about finding the door after all. It was about feeling a connection to the man who had given the world the rediscovery that Christ alone is sufficient.

Martin Luther is a hero of the faith many know little about.

Yet because of his determination to know truth, the gospel has been made more accessible to all who have followed. The results of his own personal faith journey sparked a period in history known as the Reformation, forever linking Halloween with the second greatest spiritual movement in all of mankind's history.

Journey back as Kim introduces Martin Luther and his link to Halloween through the Reformation.

Loretta Lynn may have been the coal miner's daughter, but Martin Luther was the miner's son who would change the world.

Like so many great men and women in history, there was little about his beginnings that seemed extraordinary. Born in 1483 in Germany to a poor miner and his wife, Luther's only guaranteed inheritance was what he could make of his own life. His father knew this and did the only thing he could to give his son a chance at a better life; He gave him an education. In the strict, religious environment of the Middle Ages, Luther's father enrolled him in the Latin schools of the day. Highly motivated, young Luther showed himself an excellent student, so much so that his father did what it took to send him to the University of Erfurt as the first step toward a law degree.

Luther was on track for a promising future, but it was to take more than that to make him happy. Even with the prospect of becoming a man of influence, Martin Luther seemed tormented. His commitment to religion had not left him with peace, but with a deep sense of his own inadequacy before God. He lived under the guilt of his own sins and the fear of God's judgment. That was the legacy the church had created in his life. Like the Christians around him, he tried desperately to justify himself through charitable works, devotion, pilgrimages, and good deeds, but he could never do enough to escape the sense of

God's wrath. It was in this mind-set that Luther would experience the change of his life.

Just after receiving his master's degree and entering law school, Luther was walking on campus when he was caught in a thunderstorm. Terrified, his very life in imminent danger, he threw himself on the ground and prayed to St. Anne, patron saint of miners, as he'd been taught since he was a child.

"If you save me from the lightning," he cried, "I will become a monk." It was not a pledge Luther took lightly, for when he survived, he withdrew from law school. With all of his religious doubts and questions still in place, he entered an Augustinian monastery and turned his efforts toward a doctorate of theology. Yet for all of his studies, he could not find spiritual peace. Again and again, he wrote in his diary: "How can a man find favor with God?" With his religious degree in hand, he still could not find the answer.

The church itself was protector of the Scriptures. Only those who held a position in the priesthood had access to the Bible. Had it been available to common people, it would have done them no good, for the Scriptures were in Latin. Even from his fellow priests, Luther found no help. To the contrary, he became more and more disturbed by the abuses he saw in the church, which violated what he understood from his studies of the Scriptures.

The church used fear to control the people. It preached giving money to the church for the payment of sins and the sins of their families. Religious leaders sold these "indulgences" to "guarantee" places in heaven when they died.

Angered by the corruption, Luther's frustration grew at seeing positions of leadership given out as special favors to family members. Luther stewed over the construction of newer and more opulent churches, and the encouragement of superstition. By the time Luther entered the monastery, relic and saint worship were also being promoted—in total contradiction to the Word.

Compelled in his search for the truth, he pored through his studies of the Scriptures, committing himself to an uncompromising, pious life, even engaging in self-flagellation. His body bruised and bleeding, no punishment could rid him of the guilt over his sinfulness.

Eventually, he was ordained as a priest, and Luther was sent to Wittenberg in Saxony to study and teach at a university. It was there that God began to open his eyes to the truth. And in the course of his studies, a verse confounded him: "The just shall live by his faith" (Habakkuk 2:4, NKJV). It was as if he were hit by a thunderbolt when he read it. He couldn't stop thinking about it. Could it be the key to that all-elusive question? How can a man find favor with God? Could God see man as just? Driven by his own deep need to find acceptance from God, Luther began to dig to find the truth.

With only the Spirit of God as his guide, Martin Luther uncovered what Christ Himself came to proclaim: Man can never be justified or made right with God except through belief in Jesus Christ alone. One can only accept the free gift of grace by faith, in order for God to justify him through the righteousness of Christ.

Luther could not keep this revelation to himself. The church had usurped God's role, forcing people to buy or work for the free grace God offered. Luther also discovered the original priesthood: the priesthood of all believers. By God's grace, every Christian is free to pursue a personal relationship with God through Christ, to pray and read the Bible without any mediator, and to know and worship God on his own.

These principles became the foundation for Luther's sermons from that point on, but he went further. Confronting the falsehoods at the core of the established church seemed essential, and he set about initiating discussions to bring about deep reform. To open the debate, he drew up a document of 95 points that he believed were paramount to the faith to bring the church back to its foundation. The 95 theses invited everyone willing to consider them to meet at a specific time and place for discussion and debate. Nailing them to the front door of Castle Church—something like posting a notice for a town meeting today—he called church teachings into question and began a revolution.

The day Luther is said to have posted his theses was October 31, 1517, Halloween Day. He also sent copies to a few bishops and some of his friends. At first there was little response, but then the furor erupted.

Although he may not have intended his theses to cause the maelstrom that followed, the time was ripe for change. Many were frustrated and angry over the abuses in the church, and Luther's document was the spark that began the fire. In God's sovereign plan, moveable type printing presses had just been invented, and Luther's document was promptly mass-printed and distributed.

The church resisted, but the light of truth couldn't be diminished. Three of Luther's 95 points formed the primary basis of the Reformation and consequently, our understanding of the Christian faith today.

1. "By Scripture alone": God's Word is our only certain guide for life and faith, not the teaching or traditions of the church.
2. "By faith alone": There is no other requirement for salvation.
3. "By grace alone": We are justified only through the unmerited favor of God, not saints or works or sacrifices.

Each of these truths is recognized in Jesus' statement "No one comes to the Father except through me" (John 14:6). It was Luther's own struggle to discover this truth that opened the way for the Reformation, bringing about Protestantism. It also opened a debate that resulted in Luther being called before a council to explain himself.

Dubbed the "Diet of Worms," the council derived its

moniker from the location, Worms, Germany (pronounced "Verms"). There, Luther refused to renounce the truth he had discovered and allow it to be hidden, as it had for so long. He paid a high price for standing firm: He was stripped of authority, kicked out of the church, and forced into hiding for a time.

However, even during that exile, he worked to translate the Bible into the language of his countrymen, that others might also find the truth. A spiritual reformation had begun, and it could not be stopped.

Like Castle Church hidden under scaffolding, layers of false doctrine, lies, and deception had concealed the gospel. It took the Reformation to uncover it and to restore the purity of God's Word.

Our charge is to continue to pass it on faithfully:

What you heard from me, keep as the pattern of sound teaching, with faith and love in Christ Jesus. Guard the good deposit that was entrusted to you—guard it with the help of the Holy Spirit who lives in us. (2 Timothy 1:13-14)

That also means teaching our children. Otherwise, we might lose the gospel once again.

For the time will come when men will not put up with sound doctrine. Instead, to suit their own desires, they will gather around them a great number of teachers to say what their itching ears want to hear. They will turn their ears away from the truth and turn aside to myths. (2 Timothy 4:3-4)

Reformation Day is a celebration of the rediscovery of truth and an opportunity for Christians to thank God for the chance to lead lives of faith instead of fear. How appropriate that Luther would choose Halloween—the day of commemorating those who died for the very truths he rediscovered—to make his proclamation. Commemorating Reformation Day on the last Sunday of October is especially rich with meaning as we observe the importance of faithful stewardship of the truths entrusted to us.

One way our family celebrates is with a game called "Two Truths and a Big, Fat Lie." It's a fun way to strengthen your ability in guarding the truth. With just a little preparation, you can create laughter, challenging conversation, and irreplaceable family bonding, in a game that demonstrates how important it is to know God's Word.

The game is based on the difference between spiritual truth and a "big, fat lie." It's good for playing on Reformation Day, but it's appropriate throughout the year.

This Reformation Day, take time to tell your family Martin Luther's story, remembering his search for truth, his inspiring sacrifices, and what God can do through one faithful person.

Tips for a Reformation Day Game: "Two Truths and a Big, Fat Lie"

The Game *(ages 6-12)*

The object is to make it around the board first. The Interrogator states three "facts" from the card and the player deciphers which two are "truth" and which is "a big, fat lie." If answered correctly, the player may roll the dice and move forward the appropriate number of steps. If incorrect, the player must look up the verse

---

* Significant sources for historical information taken from Philip Schaff, *History of the Christian Church* (Oak Harbor, Wash.: Logos Research Systems, Inc., 1997), and Rowland H. Bainton, *Here I Stand: A Life of Martin Luther* (Nashville: Abingdon Press, 1995).

to discover the truth. The winner of the game gets his chosen reward (see details below).

Making the Game Board

You will need the following: a 22" x 28" piece of poster board or cardboard, a yard stick, colored markers, and selected Bible verses (below).

- Lay out the poster board on a hard, even surface.
- Use the yardstick to draw a box three inches inside the perimeter of the board.
- Two inches inside that line, draw another box.
- Draw lines connecting the boxes every two inches with perpendicular lines. This will form a game board consisting of 34 2"x 2" spaces around the poster, leaving a 3" border on the outside.
- With colorful markers, write in one corner space the word "START."
- Count four spaces to the right and write, "You memorized some Bible verses. Move ahead 3 spaces." in the box.
- Count ahead another five spaces and write, "You missed Sunday school. Go back 1 space."
- Count ahead another two spaces and write, "Avoid false teaching. Move ahead 1 space."
- Count ahead another five spaces and write, "You believed a big, fat lie about God. Go back 2 spaces."
- Count ahead another two spaces and write, "You shared a truth. Move ahead 2 spaces."
- Count ahead another five spaces and write, "Forgot to read your Bible. Skip 1 turn."
- Count ahead another four spaces and write, "You learned a truth at church. Move ahead 2 spaces."
- Count ahead another space and write, "You ignored a Bible truth. Go back 3 spaces."

🍁 In the box just before the "Start" space, write, "You Win!"

🍁 Around the perimeter of the game board, creatively write these Bible verses dealing with truth and lies, or choose your own: Proverbs 14:5, Galatians 1:7, John 8:32, and Proverbs 12:17.

🍁 In the large space in the center of the game board, write in big letters, "Two Truths and a Big, Fat Lie." In smaller letters underneath it, write "[God's] worshipers must worship in spirit and in truth. John 4:24."

🍁 You will need a die and playing pieces for each person. Either take these from another game or make them out of cereal pieces, paper clips, or other items.

Making the Game Cards

Consider your children's ages. If four people or four teams are playing, you will need 30 to 50 cards. We have included several questions at the end of the book to get you started. Carefully tear out the pages and cut along the lines to create 50 game cards.

To make additional game cards:

🍁 Choose age-appropriate truths. For teens, focus on verses. For younger children, focus on Bible characters or stories.

🍁 Make your game cards out of any thick paper; 3" x 5" index cards work well.

🍁 On one side, write two truths and a lie.

🍁 Beside the two true statements, write a "T" or the word "Truth."

🍁 Beside the untrue statement, write an "L" or the word "Lie."

🍁 Write the statements so that the lie is not always in the same place on the card.

* Look at the samples provided at the end of the book for creating your questions.
* To ensure accuracy, use your Bible.
* Beside each statement, write the verse where the "truth" can be found.
* If all of the statements are from the same passage, write that passage at the bottom of the card instead of after each statement.
* Place the cards facedown in the middle of the game board.

The Rules of the Game

* Up to six people or teams may play at once.
* Give each a piece of paper and a pencil and have them write down what they would like as their prize if they win. Set some guidelines for appropriate rewards: a favorite treat, a trip to the icecream shop, a five-minute pillow fight, extending bedtime by 30 minutes, a movie, or having a friend over to spend the night.
* Each person shares his or her choice. This is fun and allows any necessary adjusting.
* Roll the die to see who begins. The one with the lowest number goes first. Game play moves clockwise.
* The player to the right of the first player is the Interrogator. He chooses a card and reads the three statements.
* The player must decide which of the three statements is the Big, Fat Lie.
* If correct, he rolls the die and moves forward the rolled number of spaces and follows the instructions as directed. If incorrect, he must look up the Bible verse and explain what the truth is; he does not roll the die.
* Play passes to the next player and proceeds until someone makes it to the last space.

🍁 The winner reads their prize and a time for the prize-giver to make good is determined.

🍁 At the end, talk briefly about how important it is to know the truth so that you will not be fooled. Read 2 Timothy 1:13.

P-R-A-Y ON THE IDOP

Pam Counts the Cost

Eighteen years, Jerry and I have committed to ministering to college students, passing on the vision of spreading the gospel throughout the world. We've trained students to go to other countries where conversion to Christ could mean a death sentence.

Yet it wasn't until I traveled to the Middle East that the real impact of persecution became personal.

Intellectually, I knew. Christians around the world were being tormented every day. I'd heard many stories from friends who had served overseas and I'd read books on the subject. Hostility toward the gospel is widespread. But in the Middle East, for the first time, I was about to encounter it face-to-face.

The country we were traveling to made conversion to any religion a person wasn't born into illegal. When we stepped off the plane, it seemed paradoxical that such a bright, cheerful place could be home to such darkness. Everywhere we went, we were greeted with smiles and curiosity. Our children had blonde hair everyone wanted to touch. This friendly country, ally of the United States, seemed to roll out the red carpet with their love of Westerners. But what they didn't love—at least not the government officials and the hard-core Muslims—was the God we brought with us. These people were suspicious, anxious that we might try to leave our God there when we went home.

Not everyone had such a closed heart. Many Muslim people were hungry to know the love of God. We were there to tell as many as would listen. The Middle-Eastern Christians who lived in that city and were willing to help us communicate and build relationships made this goal possible. Seeing their courage as they risked everything to bring their countrymen the gospel was both humbling and inspiring. More than that, our new friendships brought us face-to-face with the realities of persecution for many of those who claim Christ as their Savior.

Like Aziza. Publishing her real name could put her at risk, but she is a beautiful young woman raised in a fundamental Muslim family, who came to faith when a vision from God sent her to the Bible for answers. To have been discovered reading "a book of lies" could have meant horrendous abuse and death at the hands of her own family, so she hid her forbidden Bible in a cabinet. What she read was so compelling that she was willing to risk everything. Time after time, the Bible went mysteriously undetected, even at times when the cabinet was searched.

When she read that "all have sinned and fall short of the glory of God" (Romans 3:23), she became convinced that her own wicked heart had separated her from a holy God. Aziza knew the punishment for her sin was greater than anything her family could do to her. She believed "the wages of sin is death" (Romans 6:23). She believed with all her heart that God Himself had paid that price with His Son's life because of His great love for her. Aziza put all of her faith in His promise that "the gift of God is eternal life in Christ Jesus our Lord" (Romans 6:23). She was compelled to faith by the love of God, so deep that He would sacrifice His own Son, Jesus, for her.

From that moment on, Aziza was truly a new creature, and she never looked back. Her new faith remained a secret, but even so, she began to experience true freedom for the first time. Eventually, her family discovered the Bible and she was beaten severely and told never to look at it again. But that didn't stop Aziza because she'd found the truth. She continued to secretly read and grow stronger in her faith.

In a twist only God could arrange, Aziza married a Muslim man who was also secretly a Christian. Finally, she had someone with whom she could share her love for God. They eventually had three children and taught them the truth, but they also taught them to keep it hidden.

On one occasion, the defining moment in her family came. Aziza took her children to a wedding celebration at her parents' home. While she was out of the room, the Muslim call to prayer was sounded, and the entire group stopped to pray. Aziza's mother noticed her grandchildren did not bow in worship. She questioned one of the daughters.

"Aren't you going to pray to Allah?"

The six-year-old replied, innocently, "I only pray to the one true God."

The grandmother, recognizing this as a Christian response, became enraged and beat the child without mercy. Aziza heard the commotion and ran to her child, throwing herself over her daughter. Though she was seven months pregnant, Aziza received the brutality. She was beaten until she was presumed dead and left in the room with her children. Through supernatural intervention, they escaped home. From then on, her family threatened to kidnap the children and forcibly convert them back to Islam.

Aziza knew she would find no sympathy with the police. The only option for her and her husband was to guard the children day and night.

Heartbroken over her children for having to endure so much, Aziza wept in anguish.

"Why are you crying, Mother?" her six-year-old daughter asked. "It will be all right. They just don't know any better. They just don't know who God really is."

God was showing Aziza what it meant to forsake everything for Him. He was also impressing on her heart that He wanted her to take on the tremendous task of reaching out to other Muslim women with the gospel of Jesus Christ. But how? Unless they were working, shopping, or going to school, women could only go out accompanied by their husbands.

Yet Aziza was desperate to tell about the love she'd found. Undeterred, she began a small sewing business out of her home and began to hire other women. Motivated by the extra money, husbands would allow their wives to work for her, giving Aziza her chance. When God showed her the time was right, she shared the film, *Jesus,* with the women and told them her story. The results were phenomenal; every single woman was converted to Christ on the spot.

Today, her sewing business is also an underground Bible study. Aziza knows only too well what faith in Christ could mean for her new friends, but she also knows that no one can steal the life Christ has given them.

The persecuted church is real in our world today. I will be forever grateful for my firsthand look at what others endure for the sake of the gospel. I came home to America knowing I could play a part by fervently praying for my brothers and sisters around the world. By God's power and their faithfulness, the gospel will triumph where darkness now reigns. They need our support and intervention. For that very purpose, a day has been set aside for critical intercession. The International Day of Prayer for the Persecuted Church (IDOP) is observed on the first Sunday in November, an appropriate date as it follows on the heels of Halloween and All Saints' Day. After celebrating the heroes of the past, we pray for the heroes of our generation.

Kim and I found an opportunity to share about persecuted Christians and recognize the IDOP at the class Halloween party at our kids' Christian school. We wanted to tell what happened when the gospel made its way around the world. As "party moms" we try to offer something meaningful in the midst of the fun, so along with the snacks and favors, we also share some true stories of past heroes and some modern-day who are standing firm even while suffering for God. Thanks to resources from Voice of the Martyrs, we can tell about 27-year-old Yumei Lu and 28-year-old Xitao Zhao from China, who were arrested for starting a children's Sunday school class, each sentenced to at least seven years in prison for their commitment.

Most students can't believe people would be punished for something so innocent. They are stunned, but they are also full of compassion for these friends they have never met. They are very excited when we tell that they can write letters to these imprisoned Christians. Our fifth-graders' response was a genuine appreciation for their sacrifices, and in gratitude they became prayers instead of the ones in need of prayer. Their letters were heartfelt:

"You are so brave for telling people about Jesus in your country. I will pray for you."

"I am happy you stood up for Jesus. God bless you."

"I am sorry you are in jail because you love God so much that you wanted to preach, but I am also very proud of you."

This year, participate as a family in the International Day of Prayer for the Persecuted Church. Choose a country and find someone who is enduring hardship for the sake of the gospel. Learning of their stories will humble and inspire you. It is our privilege and our calling to "remember those in prison as if you were their fellow prisoners, and those who are mistreated as if you yourselves were suffering" (Hebrews 13:3).

Remember, and then pray.

To make the reality of the persecuted church around the world even more real, we've provided a fun, family activity at the end of this chapter.

TIPS FOR REMEMBERING THE PERSECUTED CHURCH

Pray

- 🍁 Remind your family that the *greatest* thing you can do for the persecuted church is to pray.
- 🍁 Early in the day, schedule a specific time of prayer with your family.
- 🍁 Unplug the phone.
- 🍁 Pray for the most pressing specific needs: protection, leadership, availability of Bibles, courage, boldness, etc.
- 🍁 For a good resource on the needs of the church in specific countries, we recommend the book *Operation World*, by Patrick Johnstone and Jason Mandryk.
- 🍁 Consider praying in the dark, with candles, as if in secret along with those being persecuted around the world.

Make It Personal

- 🍁 Find and research a country where the persecution of Christians is a reality. Check out Christian Solidarity Worldwide, www.cswusa.com. Learn about the history and culture, and how Christianity first came there.
- 🍁 On the night of IDOP, cook a food of that country.
- 🍁 Learn about specific brothers and sisters who are currently imprisoned—including how to write to them. See the Voice of the Martyrs Web site, www.persecution.com for a list of current prisoners (read the sample letter in the "prisoner list" at www.persecution.com and use caution when referring to specific methods of contact such as addresses and the Internet). The Web site www.christianfreedom.org is also an excellent resource for current stories.
- 🍁 Write to an imprisoned fellow believer to encourage him or her.

❧ Encourage your children to become pen pals with the child of a missionary family that your church supports or recommends.

❧ If possible, work out a way to financially support a missionary in that country.

❧ If they aren't already, get your local church involved in the IDOP.

❧ Visit the IDOP Web site for other ideas and ways to get involved: www.idop.org.

Remember

❧ Adopt a country for the year and pray for them continually.

❧ Post pictures or reminders on the refrigerator or in a common area.

❧ Once a month, write a letter to a believer imprisoned in another country.

❧ Write to your Congress representative about pressing other countries on religious freedom issues. Focus on the Family's CitizenLink Web site is a good resource of information on public policy issues: www.family.org and click on "CitizenLink."

Play "Prayer Police"

❧ To better understand the religious freedoms withheld in other countries, with this game you spend the week leading up to the IDOP citing people for "illegal religious activities."

❧ Print slips of paper that cite "reading the Bible," "praying in public," "attending unauthorized religious events," "speaking the name of God or Jesus," "wearing religious symbols or clothing," "refusing to bow to official religious policy."

🍁 Hand these citations out as violations occur.

🍁 Keep a record of citations, and at the end of the week, have family members bring citations to their "trial."

🍁 After they present their citations, read the charges. What would the punishment be in the country you are praying for? Depending on the country, citations for reading the Bible, attending one unauthorized meeting, being caught with one cross necklace, and praying in public might earn three years in prison, or death.

🍁 After each person has been "sentenced," talk about how difficult it would be to be a Christian under those circumstances and ask what they would do if such things became illegal in America.

🍁 Talk about real ways they might feel their faith is unwelcome at school, with friends, or on their sports teams.

🍁 Talk about having courage against opposition.

🍁 Read one or two stories of current-day believers suffering because they would not deny Jesus. *Jesus Freaks,* Volumes I and II, are good resources for these stories as are some of the Web sites mentioned above.

FAITH WORTH LIVING FOR

Bloodied, bruised, and broken. I'm not referring to an early church martyr, but my 11-year-old daughter, Hannah.

I really shouldn't have been surprised. Anyone who engages life as fully as Hannah Wier is bound to be dealt a few blows along the way. This time it began with a sibling collision on the trampoline. Mom can always tell that truly-hurt scream from the one that means, "You're gonna get it!" This particular blood-curdling wail sent me racing to the backyard in emergency-management mode. Sure enough, this one warranted a trip to the orthopedist.

Trampolines are not popular with doctors; I knew I was going to be asked to defend myself. As we sat in the examining room, I ran through possible things to say to avoid the "Worst Mother of the Year" title. *Let's see*, I thought. *I could say I had no idea how she got hurt, but then I would be negligent. I could say she got hurt at Pam's house on* her *trampoline, but that would implicate someone else.* There was nothing to do but tell the doctor that I found this little girl crying by the side of the road, and decided to play Good Samaritan and bring her for help.

Just then the doctor entered the room and asked, "Well, young lady, what happened to you?" Before I could clamp my hand over her mouth, Hannah blurted out, "My brother and I were on the trampoline, and he jumped up real high and came down on my arm. I think he broke it." The doctor's reaction was just what I had expected. He shook his head in shock and dismay, and then regaled me with graphic details about horrible, senseless trampoline tragedies.

"Still," he added, "as long as you have a safety net and only allow one person to jump at a time, you minimize the risks."

"We don't have a net, but we have safety rules. We can't jump more than five at a time, right, Mom?" my daughter volunteered as I pinched her good arm.

I must not have broken any actual child endangerment laws because the doctor kindly dropped the subject and moved on to the x-rays. He didn't see a break, but couldn't rule out a fracture in her elbow. A full arm splint for three weeks would be required as a precaution. Hannah thought having a splint for all her friends to sign would be cool.

Then the doctor told her baseball was out for three weeks. She couldn't believe it! Hannah was the first baseman for both her baseball and her softball teams. This was her worst-case scenario. As the doctor left, she began to explore her options.

"Mom, I *have* to play baseball. I can still catch with my left hand, and I know I could bunt with my arm in a splint. And look, the splint is bent just right for throwing. Please let me try?"

I had already made one bad decision by letting her jump on The Trampoline of Doom. How could I let her risk her life on the baseball field? So I did the responsible thing. "Just don't tell the doctor . . ."

The very next night, she took the splint for a test run at the ball park. She certainly wasn't a candidate for the most valuable player award, but she bunted, caught with precision, and with her arm splinted at a perfect right angle, fired that ball from first all the way to third base. All was well with our world, and it even appeared things were back to normal. I didn't feel guilty leaving my daughter in her father's capable hands as I left town to speak at a luncheon.

While I was gone, sharing advice on being a godly mother, my husband called me from the baseball park. "Do you want to hear something funny?" he asked. "Hannah was warming up for the game, and the ball took a bad bounce and hit her in the nose. There was blood everywhere, and they actually thought it might be broken!"

"And what would be the funny part?" I asked, stunned.

"I'm getting to that," he said, the game noise in the background. "They brought a doctor into the dugout and he said it wasn't broken. They cleaned her up and sent her out to bat. But then the pitcher beaned her in the back with a fastball."

Maybe it's that I have a vastly different sense of humor than my husband, but I wasn't laughing. Instead, I was imagining my daughter, her arm in a splint, bloody nose, lying on the ground after being mowed down by a fastball, all the really good mothers sitting in the stands talking about my neglected child. There was nothing amusing about it. I was about to instruct my husband on the definition of compassionate parenting when I heard a loud roar go up in the crowd.

I panicked. "What's happened now?"

"Hannah just scored!" he yelled. Then he added, "You have to admit, honey. It's funny. I mean, what else could possibly happen to her?"

As if in answer to the question, three days later Hannah tripped on the playground at school and sprained her ankle. Now she had crutches to add to the splint and the bandaged nose.

I often think of Hannah's harrowing week as a metaphor for the kinds of trials that are part of the Christian life. Hannah herself would be the personification of the apostle Paul's words as he described our response to such difficulties: "We are hard pressed on every side, but not crushed; perplexed, but not in despair; persecuted, but not abandoned; struck down, but not destroyed" (2 Corinthians 4:8-9). We get knocked down, but we get up again and keep going.

Sometimes petty annoyances like broken dishwashers and quirky coworkers can perplex us and make us feel struck down. Paul knew our greatest challenges would be to our faith because he experienced it firsthand. From struggles with sin to perseverance, he knew that the most relevant question was not *Am I willing to die for my faith?* but *Am I willing to live a life worthy of the faith?*

> To this end also we pray for you always, that our God will count you worthy of your calling, and fulfill every desire for goodness and the work of faith with power, so that the name of our Lord Jesus will be glorified in you, and you in Him, according to the grace of our God and the Lord Jesus Christ. (2 Thessalonians 1:11-13, NASB)

An I-think-I-can mentality is sufficient when I'm trying to resist that last chocolate cookie or fight the urge to say "I told you so" when I know I'm right. Yet there are circumstances when all the personal fortitude in the world won't suffice to overcome—especially when those challenges are spiritual.

How do we live a life worthy when God doesn't seem to be answering? What about when a friend has a tragic accident or horrible disease? How do we keep our faith when we have been falsely accused, rejected because of Christ, or abandoned by someone we love? Who do we look to then?

Of course, Christ is our first and best example. He endured the cruelest circumstances when He accepted the cross to secure our eternal life. He ensured the very faith that beckons us to live a worthy life. The fact is, though, while Jesus was fully man, He was also fully God. Is it possible for mere humans to persevere and exhibit a faith worthy of commending? According to the Bible, not only is it possible but also God has given us many examples of ordinary men and women who overcame the greatest challenges through the power of an extraordinary God.

> Therefore, since we have so great a cloud of witnesses surrounding us, let us also lay aside every encumbrance and the sin which so easily entangles us, and let us run with endurance the race that is set before us, fixing our eyes on Jesus, the author and perfecter of faith, who for the joy set before Him endured the cross, despising the shame, and has sat down at the right hand of the throne of God. For consider Him who has endured such hostility by sinners against Himself, so that you will not grow weary and lose heart. (Hebrews 12:1-3, NASB)

At the very least, this season of commemoration should inspire us not to grow weary or lose heart. We have only to look to that "great cloud of witnesses" who ran the race before us and set the pace. They lived a life worthy of their faith and finished in victory because they had their eyes fixed on Jesus, the One who authored their faith and brought it to perfection when their race was over.

By challenging the culture of their time, they lived instead by "whatever is true, whatever is honorable, whatever is right, whatever is pure, whatever is lovely, whatever is of good repute." They looked to see "if there [was] any excellence and if anything worthy of praise, [and they chose to] dwell on these things" (Philippians 4:8, NASB).

What an example they set for us! In the midst of paganism, self-centeredness, immorality, and meaningless traditions, those early Christians chose not to surrender to an empty way of life, and we don't have to either, not even when it comes to something as seemingly trivial as a holiday.

We have the privilege of following those who have gone before, but as parents, we have been given the responsibility to guide the ones who follow. We don't have to have legs of iron to strengthen them on their own walk of faith. All we have to do is put our shaky feet on the firm ground of faith while keeping our eyes on Jesus on whom our faith depends from start to finish.

Your first steps into redeeming Halloween may be shaky, but if you keep your eyes on Jesus Christ instead of your neighbors or the prevailing traditions in our culture, the ones following you will not stumble and fall, but remain strong.

As our families imitate the faith of those who kept their eyes on Christ, we can be assured that we are preparing our children to run with endurance no matter what challenges test their faith on the path of life. They, too, may be "hard pressed, perplexed, persecuted, or knocked down," but with our examples and the examples of those who went before, they will be able to get up again and keep going.

As you step out to reclaim a season with such an amazing spiritual heritage, may you discover the redeeming power of our Savior, not just at Halloween, but in every season.

T Meshach was sent to the fiery furnace. *Daniel 3:20*

L Daniel was sent to the fiery furnace. *Daniel 3:20*

T Shadrach was sent to the fiery furnace. *Daniel 3:20*

T Eve was the world's first seamstress. *Genesis 3:7*

L Eve's name means "death." *Genesis 3:20*

T Eve hid from God. *Genesis 3:8*

L God sent a plague of worms on Egypt. *Exodus 8:21*

T God sent a plague of hail on Egypt. *Exodus 9:18*

T God sent a plague of frogs on Egypt. *Exodus 8:2*

T Noah's ark was longer than a football field. *Genesis 6:15*

T Noah's ark was three stories high. *Genesis 6:16*

L Noah's ark did not have room for food. *Genesis 6:21*

L Sarah treated her maidservant kindly. *Genesis 21:10*

T Sarah had a baby at the age of 90. *Genesis 17:17*

T Sarah caused serious diseases in those around her. *Genesis 12:17*

T Rainbows go over the heads of angels. *Revelation 10:1*

L Hundreds of people saw the first rainbow. *Genesis 9:17*

T Rainbows are in the first and last books of the Bible. *Genesis 9:13, Revelation 4:3*

T The name *Esther* means "myrtle." *Esther 2:7*

T Esther was an orphan. *Esther 2:7*

L Haman had Esther's cousin killed. *Esther 7:10*

L David killed a giraffe. *1 Samuel 17:34–35*

T David killed a lion. *1 Samuel 17:34–35*

T David killed a bear. *1 Samuel 17:34–35*

T Joseph of Arimathea owned the tomb in which Jesus' body was laid. *Matthew 27:59–60*

T There was an earthquake near Jesus' tomb. *Matthew 28:2*

L Peter moved the stone from the tomb. *John 20:1*

T Thomas was known for doubting. *John 20:24–31*

L Thomas was not one of the 12 disciples. *Matthew 10:3*

T Thomas offered to die with Jesus. *John 11:16*

L The crown of thorns was a mark of honor. *Matthew 27:29*

T The governor's soldiers made the crown of thorns. *Matthew 27:27–29*

T Jesus wore the crown of thorns on His head. *Matthew 27:29*

T Cain was the world's first baby. *Genesis 4:1–2*

L Abel was Cain's older brother. *Genesis 4:1–2*

T Cain worked the soil. *Genesis 4:1–2*

T Jesus walked on the Sea of Galilee. *John 6:19*

T Jesus slept in a boat on the Sea of Galilee during a storm. *Mark 4:37–38*

L Jesus fell into the Sea of Galilee. *Matthew 14:29–31*

T Stephen saw heaven open. *Acts 7:55*

L Stephen was hung. *Acts 7:57–58*

T People gnashed their teeth at Stephen. *Acts 7:54*

T Goliath's coat weighed 125 pounds. *1 Samuel 17:5*

T Goliath wore a bronze helmet. *1 Samuel 17:5*

L Goliath's last words were, "Hey, it's a kid." *1 Samuel 17:44*

T God created light on the first day. *Genesis 1:3–5*

T God made wild animals on the sixth day. *Genesis 1:24–31*

L God made man on the seventh day. *Genesis 1:26–31*

T A star guided the wise men to Bethlehem. *Matthew 2:2*

L The wise men came from the west. *Matthew 2:1*

T The wise men brought gold, frankincense, and myrrh. *Matthew 2:11*

T Jesus was born in Bethlehem. *Luke 2:4–7*

T The first people to visit the new-born baby were the shepherds. *Luke 2:4–16*

L The wise men told the shepherds about the baby Jesus. *Luke 2:9–12*

T Jonah was upset when a worm ate his vine. *Jonah 4:6–9*

T Jonah was swallowed by a giant fish. *Jonah 1:17*

L Jonah hid in the boat from the sailors. *Jonah 1:12*

L Faith is not being sure of what we hope for. *Hebrews 11:1*

T Faith is being certain of what we do not see. *Hebrews 11:1*

T It is impossible to please God without faith. *Hebrews 11:6*

T Frogs filled the Egyptians' beds. *Exodus 8:2–6*

T Locusts destroyed every green thing in Egypt. *Exodus 10:13–15*

L All the livestock in Egypt died. *Exodus 9:6*

T There are creatures in heaven. *Revelation 5:13*

T There will be a war in heaven. *Revelation 12:7*

L The heavens contain God. *1 Kings 8:27*

T Judas betrayed Jesus. *Matthew 26:14–16*

L Jesus was betrayed by a handshake. *Matthew 26:48–49*

T The chief priests paid 30 pieces of silver to find Jesus. *Matthew 26:15*

T Satan fell like lightning from heaven. *Luke 10:18*

T Satan's name means "morning star." *Isaiah 14:12*

L Satan deceived Adam. *Genesis 3:1–7*

T John the Baptist was laid in a tomb. *Mark 6:29*

T John the Baptist was beheaded. *Mark 6:27–28*

L John the Baptist's clothes were made of wool. *Matthew 3:4*

T Jesus told a parable about a lost sheep. *Matthew 18:12–14*

L Jesus told a parable about a lost father. *Luke 15:11–32*

T Jesus told a parable about a lost coin. *Luke 15:8–10*

T Love endures forever. *Psalm 100:5*

L Fear drives out love. *1 John 4:18*

T Love is patient and kind. *1 Corinthians 13:4*

T The prodigal son wanted his father's money early. *Luke 15:11–12*

L The prodigal son invested the money and became rich. *Luke 15:13-14*

T The prodigal son's father welcomed him home. *Luke 15:17–23*

L The Ten Commandments were given on Mount Carmel. *Exodus 31:18*

T God wrote the Ten Commandments twice. *Exodus 31:18; 34:1*

T The Ten Commandments mention an ox and a donkey. *Exodus 20:17*

T The Sword of the Spirit is part of the armor of God. *Ephesians 6:17*

T The Shield of faith is part of the armor of God. *Ephesians 6:16*

L The helmet of knowledge is part of the armor of God. *Ephesians 6:12–17*

T Jesus told Satan that man cannot live by bread alone. *Matthew 4:4*

T Jesus told Satan that you should not put God to the test. *Matthew 4:7*

L Jesus told Satan that those who worship only God receive glory. *Matthew 4:10*

T Self-control is a fruit of the Spirit. *Galatians 5:23*

L Wisdom is a fruit of the Spirit. *Galatians 5:22–23*

T Gentleness is a fruit of the Spirit. *Galatians 5:23*

L Angels are people who have died and become God's helpers. *Psalm 8:4–5*

T Angels are sent by God to protect people. *Psalm 91:11*

T Angels are sent to be God's messengers. *Hebrews 1:7*

T On the cross, Jesus said, "I am thirsty." *John 19:28*

L On the cross, Jesus said, "I am hungry." *John 19:28*

T On the cross, Jesus said, "It is finished." *John 19:30*

T God promises Christians will have peace. *John 16:33*

T God promises Christians will have troubles. *John 16:33*

L God promises Christians will have success. *John 16:33*

T Christians should love their enemies. *Luke 6:27–35*

T Christians should do good things for their enemies. *Luke 6:27–35*

L Christians should rejoice when an enemy falls. *Proverbs 24:17*

T Salvation is a free gift. *Ephesians 2:8–9*

L Salvation is earned by good deeds. *Ephesians 2:8–9*

T Salvation is a result of faith. *Ephesians 2:8–9*

T Jesus taught that we should obey the government. *Romans 13:1*

L Jesus taught that Christians should stay away from non-Christians. *Matthew 28:19–20*

T Paul taught that those who don't work shouldn't eat either. *2 Thessalonians 3:10*

T God created us to do good deeds. *Ephesians 2:10*

T We should always be ready to do good deeds. *Titus 3:1,8,14*

L God saves us because of our good deeds. *Titus 3:5*

T Jesus knew He was going to die. *Luke 9:22*

T Jesus told His disciples He was going to die. *Luke 9:22*

L Jesus told His disciples He would die on a cross. *Luke 9:22*

GAME CARDS FOR "TWO TRUTHS AND A BIG, FAT LIE"

L Money is the root of all evil.
  1 Timothy 6:10

T You cannot serve God and
  money. *Matthew 6:19–24*

T Holy people should share
  money. *1 Timothy 6:18*

L Jesus said we should forgive up
  to seven times.
  Matthew 18:21–22

T Paul said to forgive the same way
  God forgives us. *Ephesians 4:32*

T Jesus said we should forgive
  everyone who has wronged us.
  Luke 11:4

T Jesus said to pray to God in
  Jesus' name. *John 14:13*

T Jesus said to pray to God as our
  Father. *Matthew 6:5–8*

L Jesus said to pray to God with
  repetitive prayers.
  Matthew 6:5–8

T The Bible says we should be like
  an ant. *Proverbs 6:6–8*

L The Bible says we should be like
  a goat. *Matthew 25:31–46*

T The Bible says we should be like
  a serpent. *Matthew 10:16*

T Enoch never died.
  Genesis 5:22–24

L Moses was buried in the
  Promised Land.
  Deuteronomy 34:4–7

T Joseph's bones were carried out
  of Egypt. *Exodus 13:19*

L Every Christian is given a sin-
  free life. *1 John 1:8–9*

T Every Christian is given a spiritual gift. *1 Corinthians 12:4–8, 11*

T Every Christian is given the
  Holy Spirit to live in him.
  Ephesians 1:13–14

T Christ will come back in the
  twinkling of an eye.
  1 Corinthians 15:51–52

L Christ will come back at the
  sound of a bell.
  1 Corinthians 15:51–52

T Christ will come back and both
  dead and living believers will be
  changed. *1 Corinthians 15:51–55*

T Jesus has gone to heaven to sit
  at His Father's right hand.
  Mark 16:19

T Jesus has gone to heaven to prepare a place for believers.
  John 14:2–3

L Jesus has gone to heaven to wait
  for Satan to give up.
  Revelation 20:10

L In heaven, it never gets dark because there is one bright sun. *Revelation 21:23*

T In heaven, angels worship God. *Revelation 7:11*

T In heaven, we will have a special name that Jesus knows. *Revelation 2:17*

T Believers will receive a crown of life in heaven. *James 1:12*

T Believers will receive a crown of righteousness in heaven. *2 Timothy 4:8*

L Believers will receive a crown of good works in heaven. *James 1:12*

$\mathcal{W}$elcome to the $\mathcal{F}$amily!

Whether you received this book as a gift, borrowed it, or purchased it yourself, we're glad you read it. It's just one of the many helpful, insightful, and encouraging resources produced by Focus on the Family.

In fact, that's what Focus on the Family is all about—providing inspiration, information, and biblically based advice to people in all stages of life.

It began in 1977 with the vision of one man, Dr. James Dobson, a licensed psychologist and author of 18 best-selling books on marriage, parenting, and family. Alarmed by the societal, political, and economic pressures that were threatening the existence of the American family, Dr. Dobson founded Focus on the Family with one employee and a once-a-week radio broadcast aired on only 36 stations.

Now an international organization, the ministry is dedicated to preserving Judeo-Christian values and strengthening and encouraging families through the life-changing message of Jesus Christ. Focus ministries reach families worldwide through 10 separate radio broadcasts, two television news features, 13 publications, 18 Web sites, and a steady series of books and award-winning films and videos for people of all ages and interests.

• • •

For more information about the ministry, or if we can be of help to your family, simply write to Focus on the Family, Colorado Springs, CO 80995 or call (800) A-FAMILY (232-6459). Friends in Canada may write Focus on the Family, PO Box 9800, Stn Terminal, Vancouver, BC V6B 4G3 or call (800) 661-9800. Visit our Web site—www.family.org—to learn more about Focus on the Family or to find out if there is an associate office in your country.

We'd love to hear from you!

Make Family Time Matter

with Resources from Focus on the Family

Redeeming the Season

For those who tell themselves each holiday season, "This year will be different," Redeeming the Season offers hope of reclaiming the spiritual significance of Christmas. Easy-to-use ideas plus the authors' own hilarious and heartwarming stories inspire readers to examine their own traditions and consider ways to make Christmas memorable. (Hardcover.)

Movie Nights for Kids

Movie Nights for Kids highlights 25 fun, interesting films that parents can use to teach powerful lessons to children. Each selection includes engaging activities, a plot summary and discussion points that strengthen a Christian worldview. This essential guide shows parents how to use contemporary movies to teach eternal truths to their children in a fun, easy way. (Paperback.)

Power of Teachable Moments

Everyday experiences present unique opportunities to teach our children about God. But too often, we're not prepared to take advantage of those times—and the moment's gone. The Power of Teachable Moments shows us how to make God real to our children right now. (Paperback.)

ENGAGING WOMEN MINISTRIES

If you enjoyed *Redeeming Halloween*, get to know more
about Pam and Kim through Engaging Women Ministries.

Through broadcasting, writing and speaking,
Engaging Women Ministries equips women to:
Explore Relevant Personal, Spiritual and Cultural Issues
Examine the Word of God for Truth
Engage in Biblical Living

Visit **engagingwomen.com**
or e-mail **info@engagingwomen.com**
to find out how this ministry can serve you through:
• "Engaging Women" Radio Program
• "Engaging Moments" Radio Commentary
• Engaging Women Retreats and Conferences
• "Engaging Giggles," Kim's Weekly Humor Column
• Other Books and Resources from Engaging Women

Log on to find out how you can arrange for Kim and Pam
to speak for your group or church, or call the
Engaging Women Conference Line, (936) 560-4888.

Kim and Pam invite you to write them at:
Kim@engagingwomen.com or Pam@engagingwomen.com

Look for these other books by Kim Wier,

Are You Talking to Me?
Every Woman's Guide to Hearing from God
and
Get a Spiritual Life!
Staying on Track in the Midst of Distractions

in your local Christian bookstore.